DESERT SCHOOL
Neville Green

In 1966 Neville Green found himself, for the first time, in the central desert area of Western Australia and in front of a class of Aboriginal children.

'I began to take stock of the vast cultural differences — what values could I as a white teacher give to Ngaanyatjarra children — what could I teach that would assist a man through stages of the tribal law or a woman in the refinement of survival strategies — questions forever present and forever unanswered.'

The Warburton community had few expectations of the teachers, for the white man's formal education system had little relevance to their children. School was not a training for work; work was what Wyalpulas did. Neither was it seen as a preparation for adult life — rather it was an unhappy interruption to the acquisition of tribal knowledge.

Desert School is about the children of Warburton Ranges, it is a sensitive insight into the evolving life, thoughts and values of the desert people. Neville Green brings considerable wisdom and knowledge to an enormous problem at the heart of black - white relations in this country and he challenges us to reconcile the fundamental importance and fragility of Aboriginal culture with the form and substance of the white man's system of education.

Neville Green was born in Perth, Western Australia, and grew up in the south-west of the state. After serving with the Royal Australian Air Force in Korea and Japan he became a teacher with the Western Australian Education Department. During this time as a teacher he was Principal at Warburton Ranges Mission school in 1966.

From 1970 to 1979 he was Superintendent of the Western Australian School for Deaf Children (Inc.). Neville Green is currently lecturing in Aboriginal education at the Western Australian College of Advanced Education.

DESERT SCHOOL

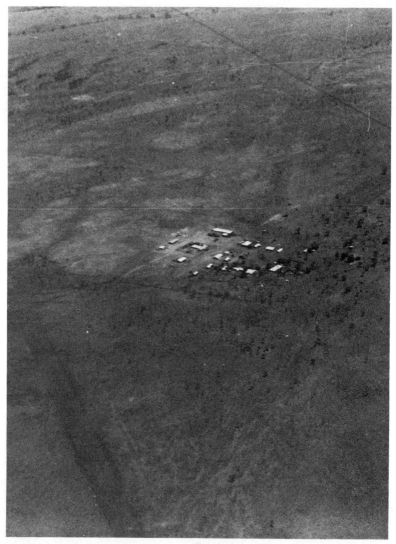

Warburton Mission, 1966. The top of the photograph is south. The school is at centre top, the children's dining-room is in front and parallel to the school, the store is the large building to the right of the dining-room and the hospital and then the church are side by side to the right of the school. The camp area is in the area immediately below the cluster of buildings and the air-strip is in the bottom left of the photograph.

DESERT SCHOOL
Neville Green

FREMANTLE ARTS CENTRE PRESS

First published 1983 by
FREMANTLE ARTS CENTRE PRESS
193 South Terrace (PO Box 320), South Fremantle
Western Australia, 6162.

Reprinted 1990

Designed by Susan Eve Barrow.

Typeset in 10/11 Press Roman and printed on 90 gsm Challenge Offset by Dix
Print, Perth, Western Australia.

National Library of Australia
Cataloguing-in-publication data

Green, Neville, 1933 –
    Desert school.

    ISBN 0 949206 86 5.

    [1]. Aborigines, Australian – Education – Western
    Australia – Warburton. I. Title.

371.97991 5099415

CONTENTS

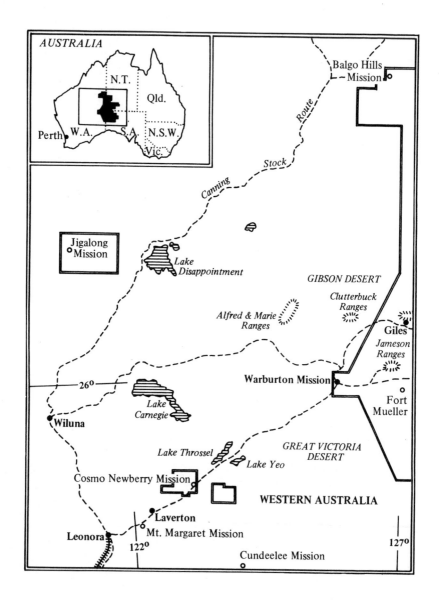

AUSTRALIA

N.T.

Qld.

Perth W.A. S.A. N.S.W.

Vic.

Balgo Hills
Mission

Stock

Route

Canning

Jigalong
Mission

Lake
Disappointment

GIBSON DESERT

Clutterbuck
Ranges

Alfred & Marie
Ranges

Giles

Jameson
Ranges

26°

Warburton Mission

Lake
Carnegie

Wiluna

Fort
Mueller

Lake Throssel

GREAT VICTORIA
DESERT

Lake Yeo

Cosmo Newberry Mission

WESTERN AUSTRALIA

Laverton

Leonora

Mt. Margaret Mission

122°

127°

Cundeelee Mission

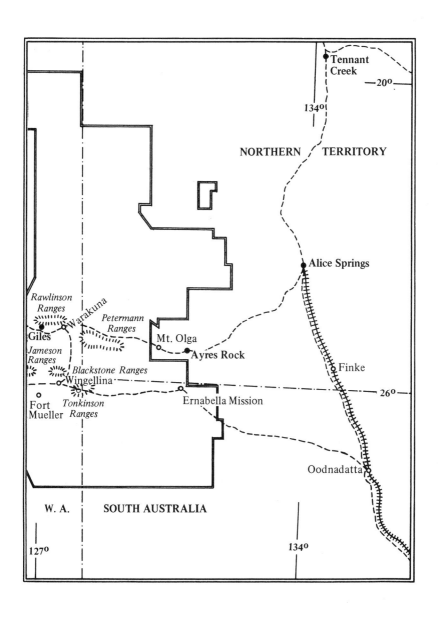

Tennant
Creek

—20°—

134°

NORTHERN TERRITORY

Alice Springs

Rawlinson
Ranges

Warakuna

Petermann
Ranges

Giles

Mt. Olga

Jameson
Ranges

Ayres Rock

Finke

Blackstone Ranges

Wingellina

—26°—

Fort
Mueller

Tonkinson
Ranges

Ernabella Mission

Oodnadatta

W. A.

SOUTH AUSTRALIA

127°

134°

ACKNOWLEDGEMENTS

Many people have assisted me in the preparation of this book and some deserve a special mention. They are: Professor Peter Tannock for the foreword; Dr Terry Williams, Dr Toby Metcalfe and Ms Delwyn Everard for editorial advice; Dr Kim Beazley for his encouragement; Miss Isobel Stanners who typed numerous drafts; the teachers of the desert schools; and finally the children and parents of Warburton Ranges who shared a very special year of my life.

The names of the Aboriginal adults and children have been changed to avoid embarrassment.

The photos which appear in the book are from my own collection and from those of C. Metcalfe and G. Waldeck.

Neville Green.

Fremantle Arts Centre Press receives financial assistance from the Western Australian Department for the Arts.

FOREWORD

This book is a personal insight into an Australian Aboriginal settlement and school. Neville Green taught in the primary school at Warburton in the central desert area of Western Australia in 1966, and returned several times in the next decade and a half. The book is a chronicle of his teaching experiences there, and some of the events that have occurred in the Warburton area since. It is a collection of examples of actual work, written and drawn, completed by the Aboriginal children in his charge. It is also a personal commentary upon and analysis of the problems associated with Aboriginal education and the juxtaposition of white and Aboriginal cultures in Australia.

For me, the most important contribution of the book is the insight which it provides — albeit through the eyes of one white man — into the evolving life and thoughts and values of the desert people, the Aborigines. Some years ago, I travelled to a similar desert community, at Cundelee, in the far east of Western Australia. There I felt acutely that I was in the midst of something ancient, sacred and fragile, and that it was a pity I had intruded. Those feelings were refreshed in the reading of Neville Green's book. He challenges us to reconcile the fundamental importance and fragility of Aboriginal culture with the form and the substance of the white man's formal education system. He challenges us, and points the way, but does not provide the answers.

There is much in this book which is funny, and much which is disturbing. The mayhem caused by the snake wriggling over the dusty ground next to the classroom, the attempts to contain and tame as a class pet the wedge-tailed eagle, and coping with the occasional incongruous flooding of the area are examples of very amusing incidents well described. Not so funny are descriptions of the trauma caused by compulsorily boarding Aboriginal students and thus separating them from family and culture, the more recent addiction of most young people in the area to petrol sniffing, and the story of the Skull Creek incident in which the Warburton aborigines were set upon by the police and were then faced with indifference and reluctance when redress was sought.

Although I believe that *Desert School* will be read with great interest by many people, it will be particularly useful for those who are teaching or preparing to teach Aboriginal children. Neville Green has much advice to offer about what kinds of tools, values and attitudes the (white) teacher of Aboriginal children needs to acquire. From my own research into the educational situation and problems of such children, I can say that I concur strongly with the thrust of that advice. I commend the book as a fascinating insight into the Aboriginal people and their culture, and a very useful if very personal primer for those who seek to become teachers of Aboriginal students.

P.D. Tannock
Chairman
Australian Schools Commission
1983

INTRODUCTION

Warburton Ranges is one of the most isolated Aboriginal communities in Australia, being more than seven hundred kilometres from any town. A United Aborigines Mission was established in the area in 1934 and by 1966 the residential population had grown to about four hundred Aboriginals and sixteen white or Wyalpula support staff, which included three school teachers.

In 1966, pupil attendance at school was very good because only those who came to school were fed by the Mission. In later years, as copper mining and social welfare money altered the local economy, the Mission passed back to the parents all the child care responsibilities. This was to have a marked effect on the education of the children, as many of the parents rarely enforced attendance.

1966 was also the year that two Ngaanyatjarra men received an unexpected bonanza from a rich pocket of copper and bought a new truck and four-wheel drive Toyota. This gave the community control of their own transport. Aboriginal law men began visiting neighbouring settlements to rethread the web of traditional culture that had been weakened by the sedentary mission existence. The Desert tribal groups then began to assess the impact of European culture on their own traditions. From this period emerges the most pressing question of the present generation of Desert people. Should western education and technology be accepted or rejected? Many elders believe that every western value that is adopted requires an Aboriginal value to be discarded.

In the 1960s the Desert populations were being exposed to unprecedented numbers of white people. Medical, psychological and educational research was conducted with the adults and children, prospectors and mining companies pegged their lands and tourists in their hundreds began to discover the Central Reserves.

In 1972 the U.A.M. Mission transferred the administration responsibilities of Warburton to the Government and to the elected Aboriginal Council. The relative stability of the Mission period gave way to restlessness and discontent caused mainly by pettiness between Government departments and a lack of leadership. The deteriorating situation resulted in two incidents that produced National headlines in 1975. In January a group of men, women and children travelling from

Warburton to Wiluna were stopped by a contingent of twenty-six policemen. The trucks were searched and several men arrested. The Aboriginals accused the police of harassment, brutality and the desecration of sacred objects. A Royal Commission investigated the claims and found the police at fault.

A second incident occurred when the Government decided to build a one and a half million dollar hospital at Warburton. The blasting of the earth which was necessary for the construction of the hospital frightened the community. Incidents of violence increased and reached a peak when the construction workers began to cut a trench across the path of the sacred kangaroo, one of the Dreamtime heroes whose travels and exploits assume a major place in the religious life of the Ngaanyatjarra. The nurses and teachers were flown out and the police brought in to restore order.

Many family groups wanted to move away from the constant conflict at Warburton and the Federal Government provided money for water bores to be sunk at the various desert locations nominated by the Ngaanyatjarra groups. This was the beginning of the outcamp movement that resulted in settlements at the Jamieson, Tonkinson, Blackstone and Rawlinson Ranges. The parents at these outcamps asked for school teachers. The provision of education in these isolated places has sparked two compelling questions — what should be taught and who should teach it?

The chapters that follow are about the children of Warburton Ranges, their traditional lifestyle, the Europeans who explored their lands and the experiences of a teacher during one year, 1966. The reader may well ask 'why wait so long to write this story?' The truth is that I wrote it sixteen years ago but never really understood then what had happened to me or to the children; even today I am not entirely sure. My work takes me to at least ten Aboriginal schools every year and many of the problems I encountered are still apparent, the culture shock is just as severe and the teachers equally unprepared for the children they will teach.

Not surprisingly, the staff turnover of such schools is high. Some teachers do not last a year, others count off the days, a few thoroughly enjoy themselves, and this is reflected in their teaching.

This book is dedicated to all teachers who find themselves facing a class of Aboriginal children and become suddenly aware of their personal and professional inadequacies.

CHAPTER ONE

The Children of Warburton

The six-seater Aztec was nearing the end of a drowsy six-hour flight from Perth, on the west coast of Australia, to Warburton Ranges, a lonely mission outpost in the arid heart of the continent.

'Should see Warburton soon', said the pilot, bringing us suddenly alert.

Then, creeping over the horizon, there appeared a few white dots which grew to take the shape of twenty or so iron-roofed buildings. As we circled to land, my co-teacher David and his wife Rosemary, returning for their second year, pointed out the main buildings to my wife Mary and our three daughters, Susan, Jennifer and Tricia.

The Aztec touched with a spurt of dust and taxied past clustered Aboriginal homes: low huts made from mulga branches and reinforced with old canvas, discarded roofing iron, flattened oil drums and rusting car doors. Even though it was forty-two degrees in the shade, men and women sat around their smouldering fires showing only a casual interest in our arrival. A billow of heavy red dust followed us along the landing strip and caught up as the little plane slewed around and stopped in front of the limp wind sock.

The pilot waited for the dust to settle before he opened the doors and assisted the women to alight. The mission staff came out in strength to meet us; the linguists, nurses and store workers, some new to the calling, others with more than thirty years in the field. The Superintendent, Dick, offered us his hand in welcome and a group of brown-skinned children with stringy blonde hair pushed close to the plane. Large brown eyes stared with eager curiosity and bare toes idly traced rambling patterns in the red dust. A smile their way brought up shy hands to cover their faces and fingers crept into their mouths as they quickly looked away.

Beyond the crowd of children were a group of women with naked infants astride their hips and a dozen or so old men carrying spears and woomeras.

Most of our clothing, food and other possessions had been forwarded to the railhead at Leonora to await the truck which would bring them the final seven hundred kilometres to the Mission. Little did we realise when we arrived at Warburton that we would still be waiting for the truck four weeks later.

The children pressed forward as our last minute packing and nondescript goods were unloaded from the recesses of the plane. A half finished model aircraft, cameras, dolls, teddy bears, a clothes iron, loaves of bread, as well as butter that was already melting through the packaging. A box of day old chicks intended as our year's egg supply drew excited cries of recognition. A Cocker spaniel pup that died a few weeks later, and a plastic bag with goldfish. These were the first fish seen by the children and in the months to follow dozens of people would visit our house just to sit on the verandah and watch the fish.

When the baggage was loaded on the mission Willeys Jeep, we clambered aboard and made the short trip to our quarters, a four-roomed aluminium house joined onto the three-roomed school. That very morning the mission women had scrubbed out the dust that had accumulated during the seven-week summer vacation and lit the kerosene refrigerators, so vital in this climate.

This was our home and in less than a week the dusty children who followed the procession and lined the fence outside, would be clean and well-dressed; their shy smiles would light wide and beautiful eyes as they rediscovered the smells of new books and the prick of long sharp pencils. As their teacher, I would find in them an innocence and sincerity that made them the most wonderful and fascinating group of children of my teaching career.

After the mission staff departed, Mary and I sat in the deep Government issue cane chairs and surveyed our new home — three bedrooms, a lounge and a kitchen/dining room. The unlined sheet metal walls would have acted like an oven but for the louvred windows which allowed some air to circulate. The girls, exhausted from the flight and the heat, slept fitfully while we gulped gallons of tepid water.

'Do you realise,' said Mary, nodding towards the girls, 'that those three are the only white children in an area the size of England?'

It was something to think about.

The next morning at first light our children were awake and eager to see the world beyond the school fence. The knowledge that the temperature could rise past forty degrees before nine a.m. prompted me to satisfy our curiosity as soon as possible, so we set out to explore the mission.

The Government employees lived on the brow of a hill while the rest of the mission staff lived on the flat and, apart from the nurses, occupied stone slab buildings that dated from the early years of the mission. These mission houses were built around an open space or compound and at one end were the crumbling mud walls of the children's dormitories, unused for the past five years.

The old mission house stood at the bottom of the slope, its outer walls of slab rock and mud bricks coated with flaking whitewash. The broad overhanging eaves gave the walls shelter from the sun and occasional storms. The roof of corrugated iron sheets was weighted down with slabs of rock and littered with sticks and stones that had been hurled there by children and adults. Towering above the house was twelve metres of

The Mission grounds. The hospital is on the left and the store is at the right.

galvanised pipe that supported the aerial for the Flying Doctor radio transmitter.

Across a broad open space from our house was the hospital. Actually it was the mission nurses' house with one room set up as a ward, but the Aboriginal patients preferred to be accommodated in a steel frame shed in the hospital yard. There, they were more at ease than in a larger building and the husbands and family members could visit with few restrictions.

Diagonally across from the school yard was the faded yellow barn-shaped iron-walled store with a yard littered with silver painted petrol drums, water pipes, old car parts and mud bricks. Just outside the store fence was an ancient hand operated petrol pump, the only one on the fifteen hundred kilometre drive between Laverton in Western Australia and Ayres Rock in the Northern Territory. But as only four or five tourist cars passed through in the course of a year there was not much demand for fuel. A broad verandah shaded the Aboriginal customers queuing at the narrow prop window. In earlier years, the prop-stick window offered the storeman a defence against an angry tribesman. He would just yank the stick, the hinged window slamming shut, and business was terminated for the day.

The Ngaanyatjarra paid cash, whilst the Wyalpula (whites) came in the back door to the store and chalked up their supplies on a monthly account.

The range of goods stocked was surprising. Bags of flour reached almost to the iron roof and rows of tinned food crammed the shelves.

Boots and belts hung amongst tins, billy cans and kerosene lamps. One end of the store was set aside as a bake-house. On baking days an old enamel washing machine bowl which substituted for a mixing tub was filled with flour by the Ngaanyatjarra women who assisted with the breadmaking. Most of the bread was sold to the white community while the Aboriginal women cooked flour damper in the ashes of the camp fires.

Once a week the store sold second-hand clothes to the women gathered around the clothing window. Old women wearing berets crocheted in wool and rabbit fur sat against the wall, their packs of dogs near at hand. The young women, some only in their late teens, stood in groups, their long hair hanging in loose hanks over their shoulders. Often there was a child slung from their hips in cloth carriers, while naked toddlers played amongst the group.

The store was only open for two hours each morning and when it closed the women wrapped their purchases into bundles to balance on their heads. Then with the infants and dogs trailing behind they returned to camp or set out for the bush to forage for extra food. Soon the mission grew quiet as Aborigines and Wyalpula withdrew into the shade of wiltjas and houses to escape the hellish sun.

The Church was a little slab rock building sheltering behind a grove of peppercorn trees. The Superintendent took the services and was at the door to welcome us on the first Sunday after our arrival. Also waiting were several Aboriginal elders, one of whom immediately wanted to know my kin group and relationship to the missionary, for in Aboriginal society there is a complex kinship system — every person has a grouping which determines whom they associate with, where they sit at ceremonies and to whom they are obliged. The missionary replied in Ngaanyatjarra and the old man was satisfied. It was only months later that I fully understood the importance of this casual exchange of information.

Inside, the Church was simply furnished with benches. The ladies sat to the left and the men to the right. Missionaries or Aborigines, it made no difference, the men sat solemnly while the women contended with the children on the other side of the aisle. The missionary saw our surprise and felt obliged to offer an explanation.

'There are certain women that men must avoid because they are classed as their mothers-in-law. It is much easier to comply with the local customs if men and women sit on opposite sides'.

The service and the hymns were presented in Ngaanyatjarra dialect and as I listened to the lesson about Christ, I wondered how much was really understood by the Ngaanyatjarra congregation, whose culture and way of life was so vastly different to that of the missionaries.

ANN'S DIARY

30 August

Next week I will go for a long holiday to the well and see lovely places with lovely trees flowers and green grass and Ill be able to go and dig some honey ants in the ground and chase the birds around and go hunting with some ladys for rabbits and goannas and bardies.

Over the weekend some people went out camping to the rock hole. When we were sitting down we saw big next upon the gum tree and they said to me climb up and see whats in the next so I did. When I was clibing I was looking down and the other girls were looking up and I said stop looking your girls I might fall down then soon I reach the next and saw three little crows and I said do you girls eat crows?

CHAPTER TWO

Traditional Lifestyle

From the air the human impact can be seen etched on the sprawling landscape. Near the mining towns the ground looks like a battlefield, pockmarked with the craters of long abandoned goldmines while further out the occasional dirt track to an oil rig or a mining survey camp serves as a reminder that the quest for minerals continues to bring strangers into the Ngaanyatjarra territory.

Beyond the goldfields and the sheep stations, the land below the wing of the plane displays sprawling dry salt lakes, like white paint blots upon the reddish brown clay. Then, a hundred thousand hectares of spinifex grass with a pretence of lush pasture give way to the iron hard mulga scrub. Finally, near the border of the Northern Territory the country changes again to become the endless lines of sand dunes that make up much of the Gibson Desert. Occasionally, ranges of low hills rise from the bed of the desert and, although small by comparison with those nearer to the coast, the flat surrounding countryside makes these hills visible for a hundred kilometres. The flat desert landscape also enabled the Ngaanyatjarra to see the smudge of Aboriginal and European campfires on the horizon and plot the transit of both friend and foe across their tribal territory.

The European explorers who ventured into this region found it a harsh and unresponsive land. Ernest Giles saw and named the Warburton Ranges in 1873 and for six weary months criss-crossed the country seeking in vain the waterholes that would have enabled his small party of four to penetrate beyond the Warburtons and reach the west coast of Australia. Later explorers and prospectors did little to endear themselves to the Ngaanyatjarra because they drained the precious water holes for their camels and horses, sometimes destroying a vital supply by trying to enlarge a rock hole with explosives. Conflict with the European intruders was not uncommon, especially when the stranger unwittingly camped near a pool or sacred site that was closely associated with the religious life of the desert people.

The arid nature of the inland forced the Ngaanyatjarra into a semi-nomadic existence. No one site carried sufficient food for a prolonged stay and no waterhole could sustain a group indefinitely. A few days or a few weeks and then the small groups would move on to the next water hole or

Ernest Giles under attack at Fort Meuller, 1873. Drawing by Stanley Berkeley.

food source. In the years before white men, the Western Desert people could not travel or live for long periods in large groups because of the scarcity of water and the lack of substantial food supplies. But they came together for ceremonies, when as many as three hundred men, women and children might camp for several days – perhaps a week – at the Rawlinson Ranges, the Clutterbucks or Warburton Ranges, then disperse in small groups until the entire population would again be moving in family hordes of less than ten persons.

The Ngaanyatjarra know their country well and there exists a bond between them and the land that goes far deeper than western concepts of pride of ownership. There is an inter-dependency that has its origins in the Dreaming. It is a personal relationship that requires a detailed knowledge of the environment and allows the Ngaanyatjarra to see the desert in friendly and familiar terms. When they are separated from their land they experience a yearning far beyond nostalgia, for it is not merely the land they leave but part of themselves.

The Aboriginal concept of the Dreaming is one of parallel time, with the past and present concurrent. By contrast European time is linear with a clear distinction between the past, the present and the future.

The Dreaming is the Aboriginal Creation, when the living creatures took on the characters of men and women and roamed Australia defining the laws of man and nature, demonstrating dances and giving man the skills and knowledge for survival. With these tasks completed, the ancestral people changed into reptiles, birds, animals, fish and geological features.

They continue in these forms to this day. Their existence is perpetuated not merely in song but in the very enactment of the Ngaanyatjarra way of life, from conception through to death.

The women gathered food every day, digging lizards from their holes, gouging desert yams from the soil, and breaking up the warrens where imported European rabbits burrowed. The environment offered an almost endless variety of small foods that could be sampled while foraging — seeds, wild onions, yams, berries, bush figs, quongdongs, birds' eggs, small reptiles, edible grubs and honey ants.

Although the women collected most of the food for the daily camp the men occasionally added the luxury of an emu or kangaroo. A kangaroo speared as it approached a waterhole would be tied in a compact bundle and be carried back to camp balanced on the man's head, leaving his hands free for his spears and woomera. The kangaroo was dropped beside the fire which had been lit with a stick brought from the morning camp site. The fur was singed from the carcass, which was then carefully covered with coals until only the blackened muzzle and stiff knee joints were visible. The family then settled down to wait, feasting on the flaccid intestines which were stripped of their contents, torn into short lengths and tossed onto the fire. Large game such as the kangaroo, were divided in accordance with tribal law.

When the camp extended over several days, a half round hut or wiltja was constructed by embedding mulga branches in the ground and interlacing the branches to form a snug dwelling. But if the camp was a transient one the women merely loosened the ground with the point of the digging stick and scraped hollow trenches for the members of the family, and between each a small fire was kindled. Sometimes a raking of ashes was spread over the bottom of the trench to warm the earth. On windy nights, a windbreak of broken branches provided the sleepers with a low shelter. Years after the branches had rotted away and the family had ceased to be, the shallow indentations left the mark of humans on the desert landscape.

Spinifex grass was cursed by the white explorers, for its spikes punctured the skins of men and horses and caused small festering sores. But to the Ngaanyatjarra it was the staff of life. As the small brown seed ripened, the women deftly stripped it from the stems and winnowed away the straw with a circular tossing action of their wooden bowls. Back at the camp, the seed was ground into a coarse flour and eaten dry or mixed with water and made into small flat shapes which dried into hard biscuits. Spinifex was also the source of kidi gum, a vital adhesive that bonded stone adzes to woomera shafts and patched holes in bowls. Clumps of spinifex were gathered and threshed with sticks to release the wax on the base of the stems which, winnowed clean, was melted and moulded into dark brown cakes of kidi.

As they walked between camps the old women lit the clumps of spinifex with their smouldering fire sticks, flushing lizards and occasional small marsupials from their refuge to be quickly despatched with a slashing

An Aboriginal woman grinding spinifex seed into flour.

chop of a digging stick.

Education for the Ngaanyatjarra child was learning the lessons for desert survival. It was a type of learning that was reinforced by daily observation and practice. Not only did the child learn of the habits of the desert creatures, he came to accept the evidence of his direct relationship with the Dreaming ancestors.

In addition there was the important knowledge gained by living a tribal lifestyle, which enabled every child to know who he was and where he stood in relation to a whole range of people.

There were some people to be avoided and others who assumed a role equal to that of his parents, and were regarded for the most part as parents. Mostly, learning resulted from involvement in community activities; building a wiltja, making a fire, hunting lizards and small game, knowing where each variety of bird nested, when it laid its eggs and how soon the young could fly beyond their reach. It was the transfer of knowledge that had accumulated over centuries of desert existence, a wealth gained through a lifestyle that archaeological evidence proves had changed little in twenty thousand years.

For the child, learning the kinship network of the entire tribal group ranked above all else. This determined future roles, marriage partners and tribal obligations. One of the earliest lessons the Ngaanyatjarra child learned was the principle of reciprocity so central to Aboriginal society. The child came to realise that every person within the tribal group had obligations to others. Every service required a payment. In most instances

The education of desert children. They are watching women making spinifex flour.

payment was made in food, because food was the most important commodity possessed by the Aborigines of the Western Desert. Very early in life, the child realised who he was and where he ranked in his relationship with all other people.

Around the campfires, he learned how decisions were made in a society lacking elected leaders, where family strength as well as a knowledge of the tribal laws, were influential in decision making.

BRETT'S DIARY

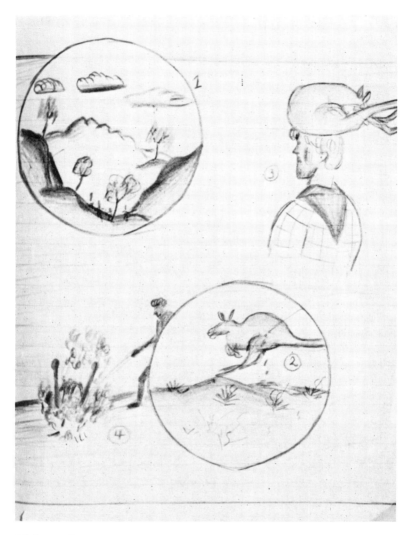

12 September
On the August holidays Bert, Gordon, Robert, Jackie and I went out long way we went out long way until we find a kangaroo Bert and Gordon said to me go around that hill. And I said No you two go round. Later Jackie and Robert saw a two kangaroos coming toward boys And I said thares a two kangaroos coming and Gordon had good spear them two was coming to close and Gordon. He let spear go and spear went right through the legs and broken his two leg and we were happy.

Will and Iris Wade with their children, about 1936.

CHAPTER THREE
Schools and Schooling

The settlement at Warburton Ranges was founded in 1934 through the efforts of Rodney Schenk, the missionary at Mt Margaret Mission, six hundred kilometres to the south.

The 'spinifex blacks', as Schenk called them, were being drawn towards the mining towns on the edge of the desert. There they rapidly succumbed to the alcohol distributed illegally in the camps. To stem the drift towards the towns, Schenk reasoned that if the desert tribes could be attracted to a mission outpost they could be proselytised, secure from the influences of alcohol and tobacco, which the missionary regarded as the two great evils of civilization.

The Chief Protector of Aborigines, A.O. Neville, was not in favour of Schenk's proposal but the increased activity of prospectors in the desert region was resulting in damage to vital waterholes and interference with the lifestyle of the desert tribes. In 1930, Harold Lasseter led an expedition into the desert in a tragic attempt to re-discover the fabled reef of gold he had originally found in 1898. Although Lasseter died in the attempt the publicity brought dozens of expeditions into the region and disquieting rumours of brutality to Aboriginal family groups began to filter through to the border towns. Adding to this hardship, 1930–1934 were years of severe drought and desert waterholes which could barely support a family for two days were being drained, dug out and even shattered with explosives by prospectors passing through.

In 1933, Will and Iris Wade answered Schenk's call and travelled across Australia to Mt Margaret. With three months' supplies loaded on camels, Wade, and two missionaries headed north-east from Mt Margaret towards the border, seeking not only Aborigines, but a sign from God to guide the choice of a site for the Mission. Near the Warburtons, Aborigines stole a bag of flour, leaving barely sufficient for their return journey to Mt Margaret. This was the awaited sign; the Warburton Ranges was agreed upon as the site of the new mission and a few months later the Wades and their two small children pitched their tent beside a well at the junction of the dry creeks, Elder and Hughes.

During 1935, mission workers explored beyond the Warburtons seeking new converts. At the Jamieson Ranges they camped within earshot of an Aboriginal encampment — one of the missionaries later recalled, in a

Desert people with the Wades, 1934.

prayer letter in the *United Aborigines Messenger:*

> *the noise was indescribable, pulsating with the very power of*
> *Satan, and devil worship, loathesome, eerie and blood curdling.*

At the close of 1936, the mission consisted of a one-roomed
corrugated iron building with a wide front verandah to provide some
afternoon shade. This was the Wade's home. Harry Lupton and his wife
who had joined the Wades, lived in a tent. A second tent served as school,
dormitory and eating quarters for the pupils. All cooking for the children
and staff was done on open fires outside the makeshift dwellings. On
Christmas Day, 1936, a flash flood swept away the tents. A visitor
described the school group in a letter to the mission publication, the
United Aborigines Messenger.

> *It was touching to see these 30 girls and boys standing naked*
> *in the rain round the fire, with their bread and jam in their*
> *hands, singing Grace.*

In 1944, after ten years of mission toil, the Wades left Warburton.
During that decade they had seen the mission established and the school
population grow, and they had also gained the love and respect of the
desert people. In the few weeks before their departure almost four
hundred tribesmen and their families gathered at the mission, and it
seemed to the Wades that every person they had ever met had come to

Will Wade teaching Christianity, 1934.

farewell them. Tragically, the great assembly was vulnerable to an unspecified epidemic which suddenly swept through the area. At the waterholes and along shaded dry creek beds entire families fell victim. Ten people died in the vicinity of the mission and uncounted numbers succumbed in the wilderness.

During the 1940s the school experienced mixed fortunes, for although the parents were still permitting the missionaries to teach the children, they were becoming more determined to exercise their own authority. In 1945, when a sick baby died at the mission house, the parents removed all the school children to the camp, and soon afterwards a flash flood demolished the mud walls of the children's dormitory. It was a time for the missionaries to close ranks in faith, for as one wrote in the *Messenger:*

> *Satan tried his utmost by every conceivable means to*
> *overthrow and close this work.*

The 1950s were years of great hardship. Whenever possible, the children were removed from their parents and placed in dormitories, but the parents, rather than have their children taken to school, were hiding them in the bush. The Government Minister of Native Welfare, the Honourable J.J. Brady, decided to use the Aborigines Act of 1905, which made the Chief Protector the legal guardian of Aborigines to the age of twenty-one years, and remove all the school age children from Warburton to Cosmo Newberry, four hundred kilometres distant, where they were to be placed in a residential school. But before the move could take place, the Education Department introduced a new policy of staffing mission schools and in 1956 the first qualified government teachers were appointed.

The early teachers found it difficult to grade the children into classes, for the expected correlation between age and proficiency in literacy and numeracy did not occur. New children arriving at the school had been allocated to the classrooms in the manner of dealing cards from a pack, to maintain an even number in each group. A school as such didn't exist and the teachers conducted classes in mud and stone buildings on different parts of the mission. The floors were only rammed clay, and after a storm the wall of one classroom collapsed and the floor became a quagmire. This schoolroom eventually became too dangerous and classes continued on the verandah of a house until the mud and slab stone truck shed could be fitted with louvre windows and converted into a classroom.

There were many problems that made a school such as Warburton unique, and classroom discipline was merely one. Within the tribal group the children were not disciplined, so at school they resisted the imposition of rules which seemed to have little or no purpose; rules which forbade the use of the home language and demanded they remain silent and seated until given permission to move. There were also problems with the parents who were angered when their children were struck by teachers, especially by the female teachers, and the school journal of the period has accounts of men trying to thrust spears through the windows at teachers and of women armed with fighting sticks pacing up and down outside the school waiting for the teachers to emerge.

In 1961 there was a sudden change in mission policy. The sheet aluminium building intended as a dormitory was transferred to the control of the Education Department and became the new school. The dormitory system was abolished and the children were placed back into the care of their families. Every school day they came up to the mission to shower, change into school uniforms and have breakfast. The mission also provided lunches and when school had finished for the day the children changed back into their camp clothes, had a light meal and returned to their families. The last of the dormitory children passed through the school in 1965 and the teachers of that period attributed their unruly behaviour to a lingering resentment of Wyalpula authority.

The new school also helped to clarify the roles of the mission and the Government, and parents began to accept school as a government institution where their children would learn European social behaviour in addition to reading and counting in English. But the relevance of western education to the desert existence was never established and the school was still dependent on the mission dining room to attract children from the camp every morning.

The most frequent disruptions to the school routine were camp fights that could quickly escalate into mob violence in the mission compound, with up to two hundred men and women embroiled in a wild melee of hitting sticks and spears.

In 1964 the principal recorded in the school journal for the

The church and government school, 1957.

thirteenth of March 1964;

> *There was a massive spear fight before school between most of the adults during which at least five people were speared. A bell was rung at 8.20 a.m. and the children were brought into the school ground where they were made to sit and watch in safety.*

In 1964 the decision was made to send the senior children, between thirteen and sixteen years, to Kalgoorlie and Norseman for secondary school education. There was some uneasiness amongst the parents but no-one really knew how to oppose such a decision, other than by a retreat to the bush. The teachers and missionaries assured the parents that their children would be safe and that they would return for the long summer vacations. Only a limited number of places were available each year and in selecting secondary school candidates the teachers were able to cull out the troublesome children as well as the high achievers. Upon arrival at Norseman and Kalgoorlie, the students were placed in segregated hostels where they slept in beds with sheets and pillows. Meals were eaten at tables set with standard cutlery and crockery and always preceded by sessions of prayer. The major concerns of the parents were that the girls selected were of a marriageable age and that supervision of their behaviour would be impossible, while the boys were of an age when they should be spending a lot of time with the teenage initiates, learning the songs and dances that were an important part of their tribal education.

Academically the experiment was doomed to failure, for the problems of learning in a second language had become cumulative. The Warburton students could not cope with anything but the most basic academic program and were channelled into trade and domestic training subjects. The girls learnt to cook on electric stoves using food and ingredients unobtainable at Warburton. The boys were occupied with metalwork and woodwork, fashioning gardening trowels, book-ends and coffee tables. Others were placed in special project classes to learn car mechanics and welding.

Initially, the Warburton children had been too awed by the town to present problems, but the weeks of the year slowly dragged on, and because the Government supplied only one free travel permit a year, the May and August vacations were spent at the hostels. Discontent grew into unrest and sometimes violence erupted both at school and in the hostel.*

The one or two years of secondary education was tolerated by the children but hardly enjoyed. At the beginning of the Christmas vacation, they returned to Warburton to merge back into camplife as though they had never been away. The only future for the boys seemed to be the promise of manhood status via the tribal law, which began with circumcision and continued throughout life with the acquisition of the Dreaming wisdom. Most of the girls returned to a camp existence and to consummate the marriages arranged by their families.

Very few of the adults educated at the mission or in towns were literate beyond writing their own names and identifying single syllable words. Most of them made a cross or a witnessed mark on documents. Those who claimed to have had some education had been to either the mission school or the mining town school, but most were reluctant to discuss it in great detail. Men remembered with affection the first schooling attempts by the early missionaries. Younger men found less joy in the memory of the dormitory system, with its separation from families, enclosure and long haranguing sessions about Christ and Satan, figures they could not explain with any clarity.

Those who had been to school in the dreary mining towns that fringed the desert recalled those days as painful memories.

They just sat us in the corner and belted the Jesus out of us if we even looked like trouble.

One teacher made us sit on the verandah before class and go through each other's hair for lice. If we found any we were

---

*   *The Warburton students continue to resist residential education. In 1978 the teacher in charge of the project class was hospitalized for several weeks after a confrontation with a Warburton boy, and a hostel refused to accommodate Warburton children because they sat on the ground and got dust on their school uniforms.*

sent home, so if we didn't like coming to school we would tell her we found some and when she chucked us out of the school we went off into the bush all day.

Most of my time at school was digging the teacher's garden and putting rocks around it.

When we got to about twelve, the teacher started to think twice about belting us in case we did him.

One teacher used to put us last on the line and stop us as we came to the door and tell us to bugger off back to camp, and then later when the cops were sniffing around for wine bottles, they'd kick us in the arse and take us back to school and then the teacher would put on an act for the police and cane us for runnin' off.

MELINDA'S DIARY

11 April
This morning we saw the mail truck coming along the road with loads on it. And also some of the people have been glowing over Wesley. And we all came to see the mail truck at the Mission.

11 May
On Saturday Ethel, May, Faye and I were making a wiltja to play, but it crash down, and we went away laughing.

12 July
Yesterday afternoon as we were going towards the camp we saw a lovely beautfull sunset. It was red, yellow, grey, pink, black, orange and also purple, green and light brown.

CHAPTER FOUR
The Transitional Life of the Ngaanyatjarra

During the first thirty years of the mission era, tribal groups in a radius of almost seven hundred kilometres were attracted to the tiny settlement. By 1966 the Aboriginal population of Warburton numbered about four hundred and most of the older men and women identified themselves with territories further into the desert which they referred to as 'my country'. Occasionally, Pitjanjatjarra families from Ernabella in South Australia, or Pintubis from the east of Docker River in the Northern Territory, or Mantjinjatjarra from Cundeelee arrived at the mission, often on foot, and made their camp in accordance with custom; usually on the side of the mission oriented towards their home country. These families might stay a few days or several months, and their children usually attended school.

The difficulties of movement to other settlements, the uncertainty of a return to the traditional tribal territory with its unpredictable water-holes held the Ngaanyatjarra at Warburton. They were people living in a state of unrest, the consequences of an existence not of their own choosing and for which there was no apparent alternative. Some families travelled south-west towards Cosmo Newberry and Laverton but this was usually determined by the availability of transport, for the Ngaanyatjarra had no vehicles of their own. The transport of Aborigines from one place to another was governed by the unwritten rules of the mission which permitted certain Aborigines, and sometimes members of their families, to travel on top of the truck operating between Warburton and Cosmo Newberry. However, this happened only if the men were needed to work at the mission or were coming home from hospital or gaol.

In 1966 two Aboriginal brothers, Tommy and Harry Sims, gained thirty thousand dollars in royalties for copper and returned to Warburton with a new Toyota four-wheel drive vehicle and a new Bedford truck. These vehicles enabled Ngaanyatjarra men to travel thousands of kilometres to ceremonies at Cundeelee, Wiluna and Jigalong or across the borders to communities in the Northern Territory and South Australia. It was the end of the spatial isolation imposed by the mission influence.

We had arrived at the beginning of that year, and although I had read several books about Aborigines, the written words were inadequate preparation for the situations that I now encountered.

The first surprise I had after my arrival was to find that almost all

An iron wiltja with food in buckets to keep it out of the reach of dogs.

the children lived in the traditional bush huts called wiltjas. This word literally translated meant shade and was a term used by all on the mission. The 'camp', as it was referred to, was actually several distinct and separate camps situated on the side of the mission facing the direction of 'their home country', that specific locality holding special significance for them. Almost a hundred wiltjas were spread about the mission.

Most of the dwellings had started out as well planned and carefully constructed wiltjas, but somewhere in the process of erection they had deteriorated into bush slums or 'humpies'. Originally the green mulga branches had been embedded about twenty-five centimetres into the hard brown earth with the leafy tops arching over, woven into an igloo-shaped hut, about two metres wide and one and a half metres high. The warmth and cosiness of the newly constructed wiltja did not last long. Fallen leaves left draughty cracks, which were patched with bits of canvas, old clothes, flattened cardboard boxes and sheets of rusting galvanised iron; all were tossed over the hut in a random order. There always seemed to be a cooking fire smouldering at the entrance to the wiltja, and, as the foundation of branches gradually disappeared as fuel for the fire, the structure became quite unstable and occasionally collapsed. Then the building process began once more.

Although the mission had electricity connected to all Wyalpula homes, no Aborigine had this facility, and the nights were spent in darkness. No-one possessed working torches, as the children left them on and wasted the batteries. A few families owned kerosene 'hurricane' lamps

Camp scene with canvas covered wiltjas.

and were able to move about at night, hugging the protective circle of light. As for the remainder, no children, and very few adults, would move beyond the faint light cast by the glow of the camp fire, fearful of the carnivorous mamu spirits of deceased men and women.

Pensions and family allowances administered through the mission were the sole income of the community, thus money did not have the same over-riding importance to the Ngaanyatjarra as it had for the Wyalpula. The mission did not issue coins smaller in denomination than twenty cents and most store products were rounded off to the nearest twenty cent unit. Yet this was not exploitive, for despite the remoteness, Aborigines could buy their food at a fair price. Coins smaller than twenty cents that came into their hands were usually discarded in the dust or given to children as play money. Shopkeepers in mining towns to the south frequently exploited the Ngaanyatjarra's lack of money skills by charging them outrageous prices and rarely giving them more than token change for paper currency.

Prams and baby strollers were unknown amongst the Ngaanyatjarra families. The baby was carried while it was in its first year — a task shared amongst the women and older girls. The ground was fraught with hazards, quite apart from the open camp fires. There were tjilku prickles, tiny mulga ants which swarmed in thousands, highly venomous mulga snakes, and centipedes and scorpions sometimes hiding in the dry wood of the camp fire. Thus the Aboriginal baby who spent much of its early life off the ground and in body contact with females never went through a crawling stage. Babies and small children were never punished and were rarely subject to any discipline. If they screamed in anger it drew laughter from the observers, and the only real nuisance in their young lives was the frequent teasing of the older brothers and sisters.

Up to the age of five most of the children were naked or wore a single garment such as a singlet, shirt or dress that merely covered their torsos. Around the camp the older boys wore shorts and usually a shirt and they were mostly bare-footed. Outside of school hours the children of Warburton dressed in the cast off clothes of urban Australia, sent to remote areas via the Church donation boxes. People in the city have strange ideas of charity and get a sense of well being by giving Aborigines and missionaries their discarded clothes, children's broken toys and even used tea bags.

The clothes provided for the children were reasonable for the purpose. The girls wore dresses that covered their knees. When the Ngaanyatjarra began school, the missionaries issued them with underwear, taking it for granted they would know how to cope. Only after questioning the strong smell of urine that lingered in the classrooms, was it discovered that the small girls were not removing their cotton pants when they went to the toilet but wetting through them. In any case they would not have learned the toilet rituals because the only toilets available to the Aboriginal children were those at the mission showers and school. For the most part the population defecated on the ground which was kept clean by the starving dogs.

There were no water taps at the Ngaanyatjarra camps and each evening the girls and women filled their buckets at the mission compound. The women used a ring of grass as a cushion and balanced the buckets on their heads, leaving their arms free for the stores and the baby.

The boys over nine years old slept in groups under the blanket of the night sky, swapping stories, watching for satellites and becoming familiar with the stars that feature in the desert legends. Others sat around the young men and gasped with wonder at the tales of life in the 'big' towns, such as Laverton and Leonora, whose combined white population was then less than six hundred people. Marlon Brando movies, seen years before, were retold to eager youngsters, whose movie experiences had been limited to school documentaries and the one religious film shown by the mission each year during the Christmas festivities.

On a bright moonlit night, the boys gathered quongdong nuts and played marble games introduced from the towns. The clamour of their excited shouting eventually exasperated groups of adults in the nearby wiltjas, who dispersed the boys to their sleeping places with a hail of rocks and abuse. For a while the youths huddled together for mutual warmth under an old coat or tattered blanket, whispering and giggling before finally falling asleep.

The girls had less freedom and although female friends often slept together enjoying each other's gossip and companionship, they were constantly under the watchful eyes of an older brother or an uncle, whose duty it was to ensure that the girls did not become involved in romantic

Susan, Jennifer and Tricia Green in an abandoned wiltja.

affairs that might jeopardize formal marriage arrangements.

One would think that desert children would have the run of the camp, but this was not so. From the earliest age, the child, whether a boy or girl, learnt that there were some people who must be avoided. There were also certain camps that were avoided because of long standing feuds between the adults. Two kilometres from the mission, along the road to Alice Springs, were several abandoned encampments — the remnants of twenty or more wiltjas rising out of the stark desert landscape like gaunt scarecrows, the mulga foliage long since fretted and rotted, the ironware transferred elsewhere. Only the frame of sticks and the burnt circle of the hearth remained.

In such places the spirits of dead people skulked and were given a wide berth by the children. Also to be avoided were the areas where the men hid their sacred ceremonial boards. At Warburton, these were often hidden under clumps of grass or in rocky crevasses. A broken branch, or a pointed rock placed vertically, were warning signals to keep women and children away. If these warnings were ignored the punishment might be a beating or even a spearing in the thigh.

The Ngaanyatjarra children's home experiences and education continually influenced their behaviour at school. Unfortunately few, if any, teachers arriving at Warburton were aware of these differences in child rearing, or the effects on classroom learning. Consequently, their initial teaching manner varied little from the models they had developed in the city.

Warburton School also typified the policy of formal education designed only for the children. It was considered 'too late' to do anything with the adults, whose adherence to their traditional customs, was also regarded as a major threat to the aims of the mission and school. A few missionaries and teachers even denigrated the traditional culture and home language, in an attempt to shame the children away from a lifestyle that was 'holding them back'.

BRETT'S DIARY

19 April
On the weekend Robert, Charlie, Mark and I were riding on a donkey. Robert said to me "Brett we go to the rockhole" and I said yes we go now.

Later Robert said to me. Brett I can see two boys coming behind us we better stop. After Mark said thats must be Benjamin and S.W. coming behind us.

9 May
On Saturday Jackie, Ben, John, Robert and I went out for a little holiday. We were having a good time Robert said we better make a smoke and I said yes we better make a smoke now.

CHAPTER FIVE

Warburton Ranges School

EXCERPTS FROM SCHOOL RECORDS 1957–1964

July 1957. Due to the arrival of many children at school during the course of the year (returning from "Walkabout") the object seemed to be to give them to the teachers almost in turn so as to retain approximately equal numbers in each classroom. This resulted in a strange classification, e.g. Miss ---- had children ranging in chronological age between 14 and 5 years.

October 1957. During morning assembly I had to chase Tom who had run towards camp, and after morning tea we found that Bill and Doris had also gone, individually. They were caught and returned. This expression of their feelings (one of either shame or hurt it appears) is becoming prevalent. I am sure that it is in no way due to the school but rather an affair in the relationships of the Wongai people themselves.

November 1958. School Collapse. Heavy rains and strong winds during the lunch-hour break flooded Miss ----'s room and pushed the wooden structure from the rock bearers on the north-west wall. Her class came to my room for the afternoon and the Mission authorities pushed the wall back, as it was on the verge of collapsing, and certainly not fit for the children to study in (apart from the wet floor). Although the wall was levered back into position, I doubt that it will stand for much longer.

July 1960. This week a school concert was organised and held successfully on Friday afternoon, the children being released at 4.00 pm. Miss ---- and the junior class moved to the old truck shed from the verandah. The truck shed has had louvres and a cement floor put in.

February 1961. School recommenced on Monday of this week. This year the children are going to live with their parents in camp, about one mile from school, instead of in "homes" on mission as they did in 1960. They will come up each morning and be fed and clothed before school and return to camp after an early tea at night. The initiation of this has meant school has started a little late in the morning and also it has been decided to have one and a quarter hours at dinner. Nearly all children are in attendance together with about 12 new admissions and classes have been fairly well settled. It is a pleasure to see that new washing sheds and toilets have been erected.

This year some children who are over fourteen will work on the mission doing various jobs associated with the store, transport, cooking, etc., and will attend school in the afternoon. Another group of older boys and girls will be given some training every week in nursing, hygiene, etc. This will be in place of normal hygiene in school.

September 1961. School was commenced on the Monday of this week with most of the children present. The school had to be closed on the previous week because a state of special emergency existed on the mission, during which all possible mission staff was needed in the hospital and for sake of public health the doctor expressed his wish that school should be closed. He also said that as children with few exceptions had all had measles it was necessary that they remain away from school for at least the first week of school. There have been approximately 20 away each day of this week with sundry after effects of the epidemic. This week documentary movie films were shown for the first time in school time, on Friday in place of usual sports period.

March 1962. Soon after morning play, there was a commotion in the middle room, due to the threatening behaviour of one of the parents, a tribal native, armed with three spears, a woomera and a tommyhawk. Apparently one of the boys of the middle room had been teasing the man's daughter, who was conspicuously absent from school today.

When the headmaster arrived on the scene, the man was about to throw a spear through the glass louvres of the middle room. At the same moment the mission superintendent arrived, who after some argument in Wongi, disarmed the man.

December 1962. Christmas celebrations were continued today with a joint effort by mission and school staff. The sports day was quite successful despite many flaws in organisation and two spear fights. One spear missed the H.M. by 18 inches! For the record it must be pointed out that this was accidental! It would be advantageous in coming years to ensure more liaison between mission and school, as for instance the location of the sports ground was not even known till 8.30 a.m. today! It was noted that everyone except the white community, was loathe to exert themselves.

February 1963. Approval was obtained by radio today for the Headmaster to collect the two lady teachers at Cosmo Newbery, a return trip of 600 miles (1000 kilometers). There would have been no opportunity for the teachers to come out as the last means of transport had broken down.

March 1963. Enrolment − 90: Average Attendance − 74: Some of the children still have to return from their holiday in the bush. It was learnt today that 'Jodi', the brightest pupil in the middle room last year, died of thirst when on the return trip to the school.

May 1963. The problems of children arriving late for school. According to the *Mission*:

(a)   the children arrive late from camp;
(b)   they are short staffed;
(c)   they have a program to get through and cannot fit it in.

According to *some missionaries* the delay is caused *not* by the showering, dressing and feeding of the children but in the extensive religious instruction carried out during the breakfast session.

The H.M. pointed out that the school should not suffer as a result of "cramming" the breakfast session. Previous suggestions made by the school staff to

(a)   alter the time-table;
(b)   help the mission with the showering, dressing and feeding the children;

had not been accepted. *Most* missionaries agree with the school staff that the time devoted to religious instruction is more than adequate as it stands; that is during each meal, i.e. three times a day, with extended sessions on Saturday and an almost continuous session on Sunday from 9–12 and 2–3.30 (average).

It seems therefore unreasonable that the school time-table should be affected in this manner.

March 1964. On Thursday a nasty incident occurred when the headmaster in trying to stop 'Ralph's' mother from hitting the smaller children, had a stick thrown at him which missed by about two feet (half a metre). The children were hastily recalled into school, it being recess time. However in the time taken to form lines and enter school, two more sticks were thrown, both of which hit the "wiltja" between the woman and the lines of children. The woman, after the children went into school, took up a position near the dining room entrance in order to attack the children at lunchtime.

Fortunately the missionaries managed to get her away before the children were dismissed for lunch. This incident followed a massive spear fight before school between most of the adults, during which at least five people were speared.

A bell was rung at 8.20 a.m. and the children were brought into the school ground where they were made to sit and watch in safety. Since a pupil was speared accidentally last year, it was thought a good idea to bring the children into an area of safety.

June 1964. Children were allowed to use the new septic toilets for the first time this week, an experience completely new to them. It has been given as a privilege to the children in the senior room only plus the four biggest boys in Miss ----'s room. Prior instruction to the girls was given by Miss ---- and to the boys by Mr ----. Children only use the toilets at the beginning of the morning and afternoon recess periods and then only when a teacher is present. Later it is hoped to let the children use the toilets unsupervised and when that stage is reached the privilege of using the toilets will be extended to the children progressively down the grades, who are at present using mission toilets.

JOAN'S DIARY

11 April
On Thursday, Sandra brought a Mountain Devil it was big and Kenneth killed it with a stick and my Mother cooked it in a red grey ashes and eat it.

18 April
On Friday we saw a picture about a three bear and they were stealing some food for the people and little girl saw the broken plate.

20 April
Yesterday afternoon June, Ethel and I went for a walk to the creek and we be digging lizard hole and we saw big one going fast to the other hole and went in. I and Kaye be look for honey ants and I dig a honey ant hole and got some honey ants and gave to Kaye.

12 September
Over the weekend we went to the place with one waterhole it was salty water and that time Kenneth and me went for a walk and I saw a Magpie and a parrot, budgie and all the other birds. They were flying above the tall gum trees and that time I saw my brother coming up to me and I said what do you want I want damper and tea because I'm hungry and he gave me a lots of died birds.

CHAPTER SIX

Preparation for School

Two days before school started I was sitting on the verandah having a quiet smoke when several Ngaanyatjarra men approached. The one in front was big, the biggest Aborigine I had seen and he had the manner of a man of importance. When he reached the fence he paused, and we looked at each other for a while. Sizing each other up would hardly be the right words, for he made two, and with a bit of help, probably three of me.

'G'day', I said, offering the men my diminishing stock of cigarettes.

'I'm Noel', the leader responded, and joined me in the shade. The others sat, prepared to let Noel be the spokesman.

For a while we just talked. Because of his status and fluency as a bilingual speaker, the missionaries hoped to give him the responsibility of the Sunday Church Services — a role which Noel obligingly filled on several occasions.

When the cigarette was almost burnt down to the butt, he said, 'When the Minister for Education was here last year we told him we didn't want any Christian headmasters, and he listened to us.'

Cigarettes were condemned by the missionaries and the fact that I smoked marked me as a non-Christian. This initial impression, and the belief that the wishes of the community appeared to have been acknowledged assisted my successful induction into the community life of Warburton Ranges.

As I talked with Noel and other men, I tried to gauge their attitudes towards the school and the teachers. During the weeks prior to leaving the city, we had been told hair raising stories about Aboriginal apathy towards education and of the violent confrontations that occurred between the parents and the teachers.

The Ngaanyatjarra expectations of the teacher were determined by either their own limited schooling, often less than three years, or if they had never been to school, by the impressions gained through campfire talk. School was not seen as a training for work; work was what Wyalpulas did. Neither was schooling regarded as a preparation for adult life. Rather it was seen as an unhappy but necessary interruption to the acquisition of tribal knowledge.

As I began to take stock of the vast cultural differences that existed between the life I had known and life as I now saw it, I began to wonder

Boys at play.

where I would start to teach and what directions I could take. What values could I as a white teacher give to Ngaanyatjarra children? This was the question forever present and forever unanswered. What could I teach that would assist a man through the stages of the tribal law or a woman in the refinement of survival strategies? Could I teach about the desert, the foods it offered; where the plants grew and when they ripened? Could I tell the stories of the Dreaming? I could do none of these things. I could hardly wander out of sight of the mission without fear of being lost. Later, on a walk through the bush, children would jokingly ask me the way back to camp and my confused responses would arouse chortles of laughter.

Not surprisingly then, the community expected of teachers no more than that their children be cared for and that they be protected from assault by older children and adults. The knowledge that the pupils were caned and struck by teachers caused resentment amongst the parents but those who had school experience had been belted too, and it came to be accepted as a part of school life, compensated to a degree by the mission food the children received. However, in later years when parents resumed the responsibility for feeding and clothing the children they became less inclined to passively accept the corporal punishment meted out by the teachers, especially by young females in the junior classrooms.

When old James stopped me later in the afternoon, and bluntly asked, 'What are you going to teach dem kids?', I thought of all the idealistic answers that had become ingrained with my college training, but somehow none seemed really appropriate to Warburton Ranges. "To

Warburton Government school, 1966.

acquaint children with their heritage through literature, song, dance, art
and social studies." (Whose heritage was I competent to teach?) "We make
them familiar with the cultures of neighbouring countries" (when few of
the children could visualise an existence beyond the desert?) "and
economic partners" (when the children's awareness of national economy
was limited to the arrival of the stores truck which by some miraculous
process acquired the goods that appeared in the store). "We teach
numeracy and literacy as survival skills for a technological society."
(Where the technological society had intruded hardly beyond rifles,
tomahawks and tinned food.)

  Nothing I had learned at Teachers' College or in my four years
teaching had prepared me for the social, educational and personal
problems I would encounter at Warburton. A tour of service duty in Japan
and Korea years before had been my introduction to a way of life vastly
different from my own, but the uniform and military arrogance had
insulated me from the alien society in a way that was impossible at
Warburton Ranges. With the first day of school only two days away I was
more than a little apprehensive, and I spent most of my free hours in the
empty classrooms wondering how I would cope.

  The long aluminium walled school was separated from our house by
a covered breezeway; it had three classrooms in line, with a shower and
toilet block at the end which was used as a storeroom, for the mission
showered the children and outdoor toilets had been built in the school
grounds.

I browsed through the cupboards to see what the last teacher had left behind and found the classroom records, including detailed listings of reading and arithmetic ages produced from standardised tests. It was a sad introduction to the school to see children with chronological ages of fifteen years reading below the level of a nine year old. The mathematics records of the children showed even greater disparity between their chronological age and their achievement levels. What was happening here? Was it moral to even consider taking standardised tests, normed on Anglo-Australian children in Australian cities, and apply these to children whose mode of living was radically different from urban dwellers, and whose native language was not English? Yet we gave these children tests in reading and spelling in English and we documented their failures.

The senior teacher's programs for five years past had been retained in the school to smooth the induction of the novice into the desert school routine. Each year's programs covered four ability levels across all subjects of the curriculum and every subject sheet was subdivided into monthly teaching units, neatly ticked with red pencil to indicate what had been presented to the class. The programs were labelled 'Grades 4, 5, 6 & 7' but the content of the programs was pitched at least two years below the designated levels.

The children's work pads had been collected and stored to save a little money from school funds. These workbooks were to become an important introduction to the school year as each child retrieved his or her books, placed them on the desk and idly turned over the pages. There would be a buzz of dialect as they recounted past experiences. It would be an opportunity for me to get to know the children and a few would shyly whisper to me the things they had learned the previous year.

I would find however that the readiness to re-do the work of the previous year changed to reluctance and uncertainty when these same children were required to learn a new skill.

The school records also gave me brief profiles of the children who were to be in the senior classroom.

STANLEY, aged 15, is the senior boy and is very co-operative. He rarely gets angry, is even mannered and most conscientious in his application to his work. He is co-operative with the teacher in class activities and should prove to be a most helpful student.

RICHARD, aged 14, is unpredictable. Occasionally he has been a tremendous help with the younger boys in the class, but his response can rapidly zoom from warm co-operation to violent opposition.

JOSEPH, aged 13. A delightful student to have in the class. He has a keen sense of humour, and shows extreme patience to the demands of the teacher. He should prove to be a tremendous asset in the year to come.

KENNETH, aged 14. When he is in a working mood he applies himself well, but on many occasions he erupts with sudden and unpredictable violence towards the teacher or other pupils. His behaviour perhaps reflects the violent nature of his family who are frequently involved in community disputes. His art work is superb.

JAMES, aged 14. Very much a loner in the classroom. Is well behaved and works well. He has a beautiful art style developing.

IAN, aged 11. Ian is one of the youngest children in the classroom. He works well and adapts quickly to a range of situations. He avoids trouble with the older children and should prove to be a most diligent student.

ADRIAN, aged 12. Another student whose moods alternate rapidly between co-operation and opposition. He has a good understanding of maths and spelling, works extremely well by himself but tends to be irritated by interruptions either from his peer group or the teacher.

FRED, aged 11. This boy is difficult to fathom. He seemed to become involved to his disadvantage, in many of the classroom disturbances of the past year. He was rarely the instigator but always seemed to get caught. Perhaps if he has a year without being involved in trouble, we could see some change in this boy.

LENNY, aged 11. Is one of the moodiest and sulkiest children in the class. Several times a week he can be heard crying in the playground with a high pitched wailing to attract the attention of his parents and relatives and bring them to the school to deal violently with someone who had responded aggressively to his sly swearing or teasing. He is a boy who needs to develop some maturity to cope with the demands of the school and community.

BRETT, aged 15. Well behaved and performs well in most subjects. He commands a great deal of respect from the younger boys.

BETTY, aged 15. Like most of the senior girls she is merely sitting out her time at school awaiting marriage. On several occasions during the past year her husband to-be has demanded that she be released from school to become his wife. Her senior position in class gives her considerable authority with the other children and on several occasions she has used her own dislike of a teacher to influence most and sometimes all the class to lapse into passive silence.

CORA, aged 14. A highly intelligent girl who should cope well if she was sent to Kalgoorlie or Norseman for secondary education. She is a bright alert student; she applies herself well to her school work and should prove a most useful member of the classroom in the year to come.

JOAN, aged 15. Like Betty, she is due to be married during the coming school year. She is not a brilliant student but her warm-hearted, co-operative nature makes up for it. She is a delightful person working with the younger children.

GLORIA, aged 14. An interesting student with a large extended family. Sometimes sulky but these moods are short-lived. Works at a good year 4 level.

ANN, aged 15. Works quite well when she is in the mood. Her passive opposition to the teacher can be as formidable as the violent responses of the boys. It is almost impossible to counter this form of obstructive behaviour.

MELINDA, aged 13. A most intelligent, co-operative and delightful student. Academically she is very close to a level that one might expect in a city grade 7 class, apart, of course, from the difficulties that mathematics seems to give her and all these children. Her reading and English language levels are all of a very high standard.

ANDREA, aged 11. This child is fairly recent to the school. She displays a delightful and impish personality. She delights in new classroom discoveries and has an infectious curiosity.

ADA, aged 11. Ada is a close friend of Andrea. The two work well sitting together and are almost inseparable outside the classroom. Ada is a very quiet worker, diligent and gives no trouble at all. She suffers from acute shyness which tends to mask a very clever intellect.

A brief profile of the remainder of the children in the classroom continued and at the end of the list there was a memo.

The children who may have presented serious problems in the coming year have been culled from the classroom list and either returned to the camp as too old to attend or recommended for transfer to the district high schools at Kalgoorlie and Norseman, in which case they would have left the mission by the time this is read.

CORA'S DIARY

17 April
Last week June mother brought a mountain devil and he said you go get a fire for with to cooking in a red grey black ashes and in a little wild we eat.

26 April
On Sunday it was a big rain and after that Ruby Helen and I went for a walk to the old road and we saw big water and we said we go away we was so cold.

16 June
This morning we saw two airplane come to Warburton to get sick lady . and with two nurse and one driver and after dinner they want to see our school.

12 September
Last night when we was asleep we heard one man growl and we got up and we saw two men fighting with spears and the rest made a big fire to watch the fight and when the fight was over we all went to sleep and I got up late.

CHAPTER SEVEN
The School Year Begins

When the school doors opened to begin the first term of 1966, three newcomers enrolled for their first formal school experience. Alan was one. Like most of the children at school he spoke only dialect, so the teachers had to have a basic Ngaanyatjarra vocabulary before we could even start the mammoth task of educating children whose experience, culture and language differed from our own.

Ninagardi — sit down!
Wiya — no
Napa — what?
Yuo — yes

Here was a beginning. Yet even these pitifully few tools could only be used in the classroom with a degree of furtiveness, for by State Law, instruction was to be given in English and teachers were instructed by the Education Department that the vernacular was to be discouraged.

In some Aboriginal schools, an involuntary exclamation of joy or anger in the home language could draw a caning for older pupils and mustard on the tongue for juniors. As a result children were disciplined to speak only English in the classroom and teaching regressed to a devitalised rote-ramming procedure that invoked no enthusiasm and very few voluntary oral responses.

Alan's decision to terminate his education occurred at the same moment that a mulga snake chose to detour through the school grounds to seek refuge under my house.

'*Lero! Lero!*' (*Lero* — snake) went out the cry from the children ambling into the school grounds.

Deciding that father was the best person to have around in a crisis, Alan raised his voice in a high pitched yell, '*Waa — Mama! Mama! Mama!*' (*Mama* — father).

The older boys, armed with sticks, surged forward in a tumult of yelling, as the snake made a brief appearance. All the younger children went inside for greater safety and control — all that is, except for Alan, who got rid of his new grey uniform and made a dash for camp. I scooped him under one arm, his clothes under the other, and took him, kicking and naked, to join his classmates.

In the meantime, more than a hundred camp people, summoned by the relayed call of '*Lero*', had rushed to the school fearful for the safety of the children. Alan's father strode into the schoolroom; two spears and a woomera in his hands and a tomahawk tucked in his belt. The father was a most interesting person. He had ten children by two wives and a few months previously he had claimed a young girl as his third wife. Despite tribal disapproval he successfully fought three duels and took the girl off to his wiltja. Now having satisfied himself that the boy was unharmed, he walked off, to the fury of Alan who now felt thoroughly betrayed and vented his frustration by throwing himself on the floor and intensifying his screams.

In the meantime, Brett had despatched the snake to the cheers of the crowd and it was left for the dogs to tear apart. Stanley rang the bell and the children lined up and marched into the classrooms to begin the school year.

How unrealistic and culturally destructive were the education programs, that we endeavoured to implement with children such as Alan? From his first day at school he became locked into an educational system organised in such a way that success would alienate him from his home and the values of his own culture. His pre-school tribal education had been conducted within close compatible groups out in the open. He had learned by observing, by listening and participating. He imitated the behaviour of those about him and rarely questioned what was told him or rejected knowledge that was offered.

As a pre-schooler, Alan had always been amongst people; he was not excluded from their company for sleep or play, or segregated from adult conversation by rooms and walls. Community living, with its drama of love and anger, tenderness and violence was bared to him. When he was hurt or in need of comfort he found solace in his mother's arms, and not in just soothing verbal reassurances, and gained an added feeling of security from his mother's breast, even though she may still have a younger child not yet weaned. But above all else there was a sense of freedom for the infant growing up in the camp, and long before he was enrolled at the school he was making important decisions about his own behaviour.

Alan now found himself cast into a totally foreign environment. Nothing in his years of socialization had prepared him for school. He found himself trapped under the roof of a building and isolated from the comforting and reassuring contact with his family. He was neatly dressed in a new grey shirt and smart grey pants, shop creases intact, while only the previous day he had been free to run without pants if he so desired. He was expected to sit at a school desk, having never before sat on a chair, and communicate in English, while at home his family spoke only Ngaanyatjarra. Within the confines of the classroom Alan found people he had been taught to avoid; a situation his family accepted only because they did not know how to oppose it.

The education system into which Alan was now locked would endeavour to develop traits foreign to Aboriginal society. He would be

Anzac Day, 1966.

rewarded for expressing individualism and for being competitive with his peer group. His teachers would endeavour to convey to him some of their own obsession with time concepts — the measurement of time and an adherence to schedules of ringing bells, subject time and meal time, story time, play time and home time. A day and a life time regulated in hours and minutes, symbolised by an old wind up enamel wall clock, its springs long gone, the dial chipped, the hands bent, spending each day propped against the corner of the blackboard. His successive teachers would seek to instil in him a concept of the future, and the desire to conserve resources for an indeterminate and unpredictable existence. He would be encouraged to develop habits of thrift and a will to work for work's sake, not for immediate food rewards, but for a money reward. Conservation of resources would become important — 'Use up that little space before starting a new page', 'don't sharpen those pencils too much', 'turn off the tap', 'don't waste', 'store it in the cupboard', 'save some for tomorrow', 'don't take them home or they will be lost'.

Home soon established itself as a place where school work was out of place. Parents and grandparents would appear as ignorant people with nothing to offer the young preparing to enter the *New Society*. Perhaps he might eventually come to regard the language of his family as inferior, their culture primitive, and their tribal ways inadequate in the face of the demands of a technological society.

My first weeks in the classroom were soul destroying as I tried to apply the teaching strategies that had proved successful in the city. Here my witticisms drew no responses and my joking manner was regarded with suspicion, causing the children to withdraw. A direct question would cause a child to look away or giggle nervously behind her hands. The snappy routine of maths drills around the classroom became a detached monologue as the children sat and stared back at me in silence. Oral activities involving the entire group were more acceptable and on occasions, such as the morning opening sessions, we sang through every song and nursery rhyme – European of course – that we could remember. *We* was the operative word. If I stood out the front and said "one, two" – and expected the class to continue – they didn't. I had to start the singing and sing with the children. If I stopped, they stopped. Furthermore I had to rely on the previous teacher's records to discover which songs the children might know, for no child would volunteer a song title above a barely audible whisper that was rarely repeated. At that stage of the year I could neither identify the origin of a whispered response, or understand, without great difficulty, the meaning of the English words masked, as they were, by the Ngaanyatjarra accents.

What was wrong with my teaching? I was more than puzzled – I was frustrated and dismayed. Had I arrived at Warburton direct from college, the children's failure to respond – and I saw it then as the children's failure – would have totally crushed my confidence. An effective teacher must have both confidence and a belief in the rightness of what is being taught. I was losing. I was getting nowhere and becoming both culturally and psychologically disoriented. I left the classroom each day heavy with the conviction I had taught the children nothing, and even worse I began to approach the new day with a growing pessimism that I would never achieve anything. Yet I couldn't blame the children altogether, because I thoroughly enjoyed their company, but there was a nagging fear that unless the situation changed, my frustrations might be directed towards them as resentment and anger. The public so often regards school as a nice place where teachers radiate smiles and dispense knowledge like cod liver oil on a spoon; given regularly it must unquestionably do some good. But it can be a hell of a job if the teacher is not communicating effectively with the children, and teaching at Warburton was rapidly becoming a hell of a job.

I had always revelled in my role of teacher and held a high opinion of my ability to enthuse children. I was unprepared for the changes that occurred in some of the children. They were knowledgeable chatterboxes during the informal interactions that took place in my garden or on bush walks, but became shy and unresponsive in the classroom. The same children refused to direct any communication towards me, averted their heads to avoid visual encounters, became sullen at my persistent questioning and reacted with anger and violent expressions if I was too critical of their work.

It was apparent that schooling was not education for the Warburton child. Classroom was a vacuum in which living ceased for a few hours each day. Beyond the classroom there was a rich array of social interaction, where all the activities of a community were on public display – the anger,

The senior classroom at Warburton, 1966.

laughter and fights, the screams of new born children and the mutterings of the senile. The child raised in such an open environment developed a deep understanding of the relationships of all that was happening — except for school.

It was time to stand off, to view objectively my teaching and myself; to analyse my failures; to define new objectives and apply teaching strategies that were more appropriate to children in a desert school. In the months that followed I experimented with ways of utilising the out-of-doors environment — so that the activities of the classroom would have relevance for camp life. I was yet to learn that the children have concepts of time and dimension that functioned on a different plane to European concepts; my problem, and one which I never solved, was how to mesh the two in meaningful classroom activities.

However, by trying to understand the child I came to realise that the early socialization made it difficult, and sometimes impossible for traditional Western teaching methods to succeed with desert children. I was soon convinced that it was easier for me to modify the content and strategies of school education than it was to overthrow the child's traditional learning and home values.

Adding to the problems of the first weeks was the effect of the oppressive heat. By afternoon everyone was drowsy. At the camp and in the shade of the store, people were sleeping and many of the mission staff were having a quiet doze. Only the teachers plodded on, forcing reluctant children to stay awake. If I opened the windows the searing desert heat drifted in and if I left them closed — the air was stifling. At two o'clock on the first day the temperature passed forty degrees and was still climbing so I rang the home bell and the children tumbled out of doors, glad to escape into the open.

After that first day I realised it would be impossible to teach some afternoons so I just talked about where I had been. The children gathered close and whispered questions about my family. They were even more interested when I said that I had eleven younger brothers and sisters and that my father had had two wives. I talked about my brothers and my sisters and their children, and certainly my large family seemed to give me some new status in the eyes of the children. I showed them photographs of my family as children. It was not a well off middle class story-book family but the product of depression and poverty. Perhaps my background made it easier for me to accept people who had no measurable wealth.

During these sessions I began to learn something new about myself. As teachers we tend to shut ourselves off from children and keep our private lives and our past histories separate from the classroom. We close the door on ourselves and in so doing we close the door on the children. We do not invite children into our own lives, and we do not encourage them to invite us into theirs. But I found the children were interested in kinships and family affairs, and I encouraged their interest and they began to ask questions and talk to me. These were delightful intimate times and in the weeks ahead they would gradually tell me, a little at a time, about themselves and their families. I learned that many of the things Anglo-Australian children regarded as important were not valued here. Most of the children knew how old they were but none knew their date of birth. Aboriginal people did not use personal names indiscriminately the way Wyalpulas did — so they readily accepted the European names that missionaries gave them. I learnt all the mission names in the first week but I knew only five Aboriginal names by the end of the year.

ANDREA'S DIARY

27 July
Yesterday, Linda, Mummy Michael and I went for a walk for goanna and came back. When it was moonlight I saw Richard coming to tell us to go and see the slide of Northern Territory peoples. After, Mummy said Richard you want a goanna tail and Richard said Yes.

8 August
Over the week-end all the people went to Wunda for picnic and saw two emus running fast and Uncle Noel was chasing fast and one was outside and one emu inside and we saw the turkey going far and we stopped and Clem shoot it in the heart. After we saw sandhill when we past that we saw the hills and saw rabbits all over the place and Daddy chasing the Kangaroo to another hill.

CHAPTER EIGHT

Settling In

The week after our arrival dysentery struck our family and refused to respond to the barrage of treatments the hospital nurses offered. The missionaries assured us that it was only the water and when our systems became accustomed to it, we would have no further trouble. The water was terrible. A windmill pumped it into a five thousand gallon open tank outside our house.

David, my co-teacher, and I decided to investigate the contents. A dead bird was floating in a green slime on top of the water and there was twenty centimetres of muck at the bottom. The missionaries didn't seem perturbed about it, observing that it was vastly superior to some of the waterholes that the Ngaanyatjarra used. Nevertheless, David and I spent the day bailing out the muck and scrubbing the walls of the tank.

The sickness had brought with it a state of depression — a sense of being imprisoned by the desert. Adding to our misery was the news that our supplies and luggage had been delayed and it might be two more weeks before the truck got through. As events turned out it was three weeks. The children and Mary were in the early stages of culture shock and missing the familiar cues of city life; the cars, the smell of gasoline burning, fish and chips on Friday night, green lawns, fresh food, feeling clean and feeling cool, the sounds of buses, car brakes and crowds!

To escape from the mission we decided to walk to Brown Range three kilometres distant. It wasn't really a range, merely a long rocky outcrop associated with a goanna story of the Dreamtime. But it gave us an objective.

From the crest of Brown Range we looked back towards the settlement. The iron rooves of the mission buildings glistened in the distance and the steady, winking flash of the sunlight reflected on the blades of the windmill. The camp area was bare of trees, evidence of three decades of camping. The desert ecology could not withstand the prolonged camping of humans and the trees that took two generations to grow were rapidly chopped out. The ground left bare, was stirred by the passage of dogs and scurrying feet — and took on a layer of fine dust. The summer wind sucked up the land in mighty clouds of dust and scattered it across the wasteland. In winter, no trees checked the icy wind and softened its path through the camps. The old people huddled together with their dogs

The flood of 1966. The church is on the left and the superintendent's house on the right.

while the tin on the wiltjas thudded with a steady monotonous clank that destroyed sleep and evoked fears of the carnivorous mamu spirits of the dead, that waited beyond the pale of the flickering firelight.

Several times a year, when the rain clouds shed their load on the rock driven slopes of the Warburton Ranges no trees remained as a bulwark to the flood and the camp became awash with the sweep of waters that caked blankets, clothes and food with a layer of deep red mud.

We could only get radio reception for a brief period after sunset and we heard on the regional news the night before our walk to Brown Range that rains were moving inland. Now from the range we saw white puff ball clouds materialize in a clear sky and spread across the horizon and this sent us hurrying back to the mission. By late afternoon, the sky hung black and the fading rays of the sun etched the whiteness of the river gums against the velvet hills.

Before nightfall we brought out all our pots, pans and cups to collect the overflow rain from the roof so we could fill the bath with a rare treasure — fresh water; to be able to make tea that tasted like tea; to be able to feel clean after a wash — oh what a luxury to look forward to!

About eleven at night, the first exploring drops exploded on the aluminium roof. A flat emotionless PANG! . . . PANG! with a quickening tempo like the merging of many drummers until the whole percussion orchestra became an hour after hour roar. Long into the early hours it continued until we were awakened by the sudden silence.

The missionaries on the flat land below us first became aware of the rising flood waters when a worker rolled over in the darkness of his mud and stone hut and jerked suddenly awake as his hand flopped into the current running under his bed.

He groped in the dark for the hurricane lamp or a 'big Jim' torch and searched along the walls for shoes that were bobbing their way towards the doorway. He splashed in knee-high water to get the kerosene refrigerator units out of the mud and lifted the two-way radio above the water level to safeguard the mission's only link with the outside world. Trunks, cases, bedding, and the flotsam of household goods bobbed from room to room with the movement of the floodwaters.

We knew none of this until the sounds of activity at first light brought us outside. From our vantage point on high land it seemed as though a river stretched to the hills. Aborigines were still coming in from the camp, strung out in lines, wading through water. The women were loaded down with children and camp equipment while the men with sodden grey blankets across their heads and shoulders carried rifles and spears.

All day the Ngaanyatjarra clustered around the settlement. By mid-afternoon the sun had recovered most of its heat. The waters soaked into the ground and rapidly firmed on the surface for walking — but it continued treacherous for vehicles for two more weeks, which delayed the supply truck with our luggage and provisions.

Friday afternoon in Government schools was traditionally reserved for sport. However, at Warburton, the sole equipment being one football and one basketball, which I had brought with me from Perth, there were certain practical limitations. The boys kicked the football along the rocky roadway between the school and the dining room, while the girls played a few ball games. I also brought up a softball bat and ball and introduced this sport to Warburton, and as long as I fetched the ball when it was hit into the scrub, everyone enjoyed a rudimentary form of the game.

Lack of finance was a major problem — the government provided only three dollars per child per year with which all text books, pencils and art materials had to be purchased. In most schools the Parents and Citizens committee raised money for projectors, duplicators and sports equipment, but the principals of Aboriginal schools had to juggle the three dollars per head as best they could, and beg the rest from city schools and sporting clubs.

During February the temperature crept up over thirty-eight degrees by nine a.m. every morning and often reached forty-three degrees in the mid-day shade. As it hovered over forty the teachers and children began to anticipate an early dismissal, as by regulation, when all attempts to reduce the temperature below forty degrees failed, the principal could close the school for the day. Two weeks after the flood there was still water in the deeper holes of the creek and Stanley approached me hesitantly.

'Good swim place close-up, Sir. Only take maybe a few minutes to get there'.

Regulated time and measured distance seemed to have little relevance for these children. No-one apart from the Wyalpula wore watches, or had radios. The Aborigines couldn't understand our obsession for categorising everything into measurable quantities, whether it was time, distance, weight or human existence. One day when I asked who had done an obviously ancient rock etching, my informant blandly replied with typical logic, 'Someone who was here before us'.

Our concept of time was not important to the Warburton people, although their lives were becoming increasingly ordered by our quantitative distributions – the store opened at half past ten and people would wait at the closed window around this time because this was the part of the morning when it usually opened. Children came to the dining room because they were awake and hungry – not because school was due to commence at nine o'clock.

When Stanley put his proposal to me, the time and distance seemed quite reasonable and were certainly within our afternoon time schedule. I didn't think to question the term 'close-up', which in this instance meant a two hour walk.

'Okay!' I replied, 'we'll go swimming after lunch. I'll see the mission.'

While the children eagerly gulped down their food, excited at the prospect of an afternoon away from the classroom, the missionaries brought out the one thing that I had overlooked – bathing costumes – a strange collection of fashions that had been culled from the mission used clothing bags over the years. This was a rare opportunity for dressing up and the children disappeared into the change rooms, to emerge shyly, dressed in the strange garb, laughing behind their hands in their embarrassment as they paraded in the closest thing to nakedness that the mission tolerated.

Assuring the dining room that we would be back by four, we set out along the broad highway of dust that was our airstrip. Our approach to the camp was challenged at the first cluster of wiltjas by scrawny dogs who leapt out of the shadow of tattered trees. The women flung questions at the children who replied with impatient monosyllabic answers in dialect. Old people, their lined bodies living testimonies to decades of the savage desert existence, sat beside the fires that burned at the entrance to every wiltja. In the manner of old people, they faintly waved half bent arms, their heads nodding to the rhythm of their laughter. Everywhere about the camp lay empty food tins, that had been smashed open with rocks or tomahawks and the contents extracted with sticks or fingers, and the tins then scattered by the dogs.

Our path crossed the tracks of some young men returning to camp. A single shot rifle dropped like a thin crossbar from one man's clenched fist while with the other hand he signed to the children. The index finger and thumb pointed to make a 'V' against the closed fingers and twisted rapidly in a boring action clearly relaying the news that the hunt had not been successful. This was the wiyatu or 'nothing' sign that saved many lengthy explanations and occasionally a fruitless walk. In the following months I would often pass a man reclining in the shade of a tree on my way to the store, who would wordlessly point two crooked fingers at his nose. I responded in a complimentary silence with a rapid wiyatu sign denoting that I had no cigarettes for sale. In this way the man did not lose status in the asking and I did not offend by my refusal.

The little ones clung to the teachers who trailed behind the demanding pace set by the senior boys and girls. Inquisitive fingers tested the skin on our hands and delighted in ruffling the hair on our arms, to discover if such textures were real.

About a kilometre from the range, the boys lengthened their already punishing stride and headed straight for a reedy patch of swamp that marked the location of fresh water. Utilising stubby pieces of stick and their fingers they soon dug a hole about half a metre deep. They called me over and proudly showed me the four inches of dubious water that skulked in the sandy bottom of the pit.

'What's the hurry?', I enquired, as I sank down amongst the cool reeds.

'Boys drink first!', explained Stanley with typical simplicity. It was a traditional right. The girls were aware of it and made no effort to challenge what had always been done.

Some of the girls continued on to the swimming pool, preferring to drink there. Others sat patiently some distance apart, utilising their time in restless food gathering that never seemed to cease. Their fingers sifted the sand on the banks, digging up small, slightly tart bulbs that they called wild onion.

Suddenly Stanley realised that I had not drunk and a rusty jam tin was offered for my convenience. The water had a brackish, almost salt taste and as I swilled a small quantity in my mouth I wondered if this was the soak of bitter water that the explorer Giles had found in this creek almost a hundred years before when he gave it the name of Elder. Later in the week we talked about Giles and other explorers and their obsession with marking trees and rocks with initials and dates of their arrivals. The children were quite interested in this and during the months that followed, they frequently reported the discovery of names at distant waterholes.

Where dates were visible we tried to deduce whether they were explorers, prospectors, missionaries or tourists. When these were nearby or I could get transport, we would pack lunch and the children would take us to a site. It was a sharing of experiences that recognised the knowledge that each of us brought to a new situation, and I wondered how I could apply this principle to my classroom teaching.

When we at last reached the creek and scrambled down the banks to the fine sand and smooth round stones, it was so cool that it was like tumbling into an air-conditioned room. The glistening white trunks of the river gums stretched upwards to a canopy of dense, pale green foliage that vibrated with small finches. Further up the creek, a flock of crested pigeons took sudden alarm and the rapid whirring of their flight echoed back to us.

A hundred brown children snaked their way along the creek bed, pulling on the low branches, leaping across the sunblasted patches of sand to splash briefly in a welcome pool, then run on again, through a string of shallow pools that wound back into the foothills. Their screams echoed up and down the creek, bringing the place alive with the sounds of laughter.

During our stay at Warburton this was the only occasion when there was sufficient water in the creeks to go swimming — but it was talked about by our children many months later as: 'That time when it rained. Remember?'

GLORIA'S DIARY

7 July
Last night Connie and I were sleeping inside the iron wiltja and it was warm. later on we heard dog coming towards me and Connie.

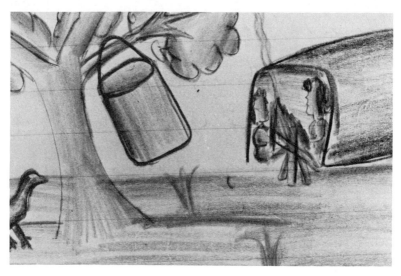

30 September
Last night I went to Harolds places and his places was made of iron. He and Phills were sitting next to the fire. And Harold gave me a cup of tea. And he was telling a story about his self when he was at home.

CHAPTER NINE
Discovering What and How to Teach

Every teacher in the school system received a neatly bound volume of subject syllabi that set out clearly and concisely what would be taught, and to whom it would be taught. Years after I left Warburton I would flush with embarrassment when I looked at photographs of those days, and like beacons on the back wall were the charts of the Pinta, Nina and Santa-Maria — because Columbus was on the curriculum for Year 4. Without even considering that these children had never even seen the sea — I taught them about Columbus and was well on the way towards Vasco Da Gama and Magellan when I began to realise that I would have to devise a program that was more relevant to the experiences and future needs of these children.

Money was a teaching area of great difficulty in Aboriginal schools and Warburton was no exception, so I decided to tackle that first.

Why teach money in a society where two-thirds of the population have no immediate opportunity to use it? That was a question that bothered me. It became even more of a conscience teaser when I tried to extend the examples beyond the range of the money available at the school shop. Aboriginal parents, when they have money, are exceedingly generous, and when they were in the towns it was not uncommon for their children to be given a ten dollar note to buy icecreams and then walk away from the counter without waiting for change. Adult Aborigines were equally vulnerable to exploitation by dishonest people. I hoped that by the end of the year the children would know the exact change from a dollar for small purchases and be able to estimate the approximate change from up to ten dollars. Very few shoppers know precisely what their change must be, but most of us know if it looks wrong when it is placed in our hand. I thought this would be a realistic approach and by mid-year I could see real progress, but mathematics continued to be a difficult subject to teach.

Almost everything in the mission store was sold in units of twenty cents. By dispensing with the smaller coins a great deal of confusion was avoided. However, in the school the children had to learn to use the whole range of Australian currency, so we started our own shop in a corner of the room, using a variety of foodstuffs lent by the store and supplemented from our personal stock.

Boys learning to play musette.

Commencing with paper cut-outs of money, the class rapidly progressed to real currency, buying goods at marked prices, giving and checking change. By the end of the year a high degree of proficiency had been achieved by these children who normally never got to handle any money. During the course of the experiment, there was over a hundred dollars divided amongst the groups and I lost only twenty cents, a fact emphasising either the extraordinary honesty of desert children or the lack of importance that money had in that community.

One day as I was unpacking a box of school supplies, a plastic flute fell to the floor.

'Napa, Sir?' 'What's that, Sir?', asked Betty.

'A musette', I replied, and demonstrated with a simple nursery rhyme.

Sensing their interest I gave Stanley, Joseph, Betty and Cora an instrument each and sent them outside to practise. Their aptitude for music was astounding and within two weeks I had sent south for sufficient musettes for the whole class. Initially, reading music posed something of a problem, but it was eventually solved by making a hundred paper musette shapes, blocking out the fingering for the basic notes and arranging these on a large press-board staff. Within a week all the children could play a simple nursery rhyme and soon they had quite a repertoire of popular songs. By the end of the year most could read music and had graduated to the Dulcet recorder. A new dimension of learning had been introduced into the desert classroom and I was elated with the results. Traditional Aboriginal learning is based on observation and participation and this was easily applied to music.

At times the little instruments found their way into the deep pockets of school trousers and occasionally in the quiet of the evening I could hear above the sounds of camp life the haunting notes of a plastic flute drifting up to the mission. And I would make a mental note to check the desks in the morning.

There are always occasions when learning another language can produce humorous situations, especially when a new word has an altogether different meaning in the home language.

During a visit by the police patrol which called at the mission about four times a year, we discussed Australian law, courts and gaol.

'What's gaol, sir?' asked Joseph.

How could I explain?

Rather than talk in an abstract manner, I decided to simulate a courtroom scene by modifying a child play and involve every member of the class in the drama. We had a judge, defence, attorney and prosecutor. We empanelled our twelve good men and true, and the remainder of the class were to be a participating audience. But whenever I referred to the jury, the rest of the class erupted into peals of laughter — to the obvious discomfit of the jurymen. Ken and Adrian had to be restrained from leaping out of the jury box to punch the main tormentors.

That afternoon I tackled Billy. 'What does jury mean?' I asked.

He was a little startled, so I explained the problem. He listened attentively and sat for a while chuckling to himself before he said, 'Dem kids think you swearing *kalu tjuri.* Whee, very bad for teacher to swear', and he ambled over to the store to relay the joke to the other men.

I went with him and when the hilarity had settled, the men explained patiently that every time I pointed to the selected few and said, 'You are the jury', the class saw the similarity to their word *kalu tjuri* which translated to English was *skinless penis.*

Those who work in outback regions sometimes scoff at the suggestion that Aboriginal children can really develop a concept of beauty. But such people never see beyond the ugliness of imposed poverty. They never realise that the children of the desert see every facet of nature's beauty and their art reveals their magnificent affinity with the subtle moods of nature. Even more important, teachers have not contaminated the child's artistic expression with trite symbols. City children are quickly taught that people can be reduced to stick figures, that trees look like icecream cones, and clouds are always white and hills a lumpy brown or green. The language barrier saved these outback children from such influences. They painted what they saw; red clouds or black; hills that were yellow or blue, capturing fleeting moments of intrinsic beauty. This did not mean that all were great artists, but they were enthusiastic. I noticed one day that several children were drawing sunset scenes in which the foreground was illuminated. We discussed this in a problem posing situation.

'What can you see when the sun goes down? Shut your eyes and imagine it.' That night I sent them home to look at the camp when there was no sun and see what colours were visible.

On my class timetable I allotted all the skill subjects — reading, writing, reading and spelling to the morning session, as much to discipline myself, as to ensure that all subjects had their even measure. Nevertheless there were many days when I dispensed with the timetable and tuned into the ideas that were paramount at that moment. So when the children marched into the classroom next morning we opened the day with art. What an incredible revelation as the absolute vitality of Aboriginal life in the evening camps appeared silhouetted against glowing fires and the setting sun! The people and their chores; the fights; the hunters returning to camp; the trucks arriving home from a ceremony. The children began to look anew at their own customs and give these expression through school subjects such as art, creative writing, science, social studies and craft. It was the beginning of my conviction that the child's culture and lifestyle must be reflected in the school curriculum for education to have meaning. Gradually we began to break the barriers that made school a place where children only learnt Wyalpula business.

At least once a week we had a walk session that gave me a chance to take the classroom into the bush and bring some of it back. Every bush walk with the children was interspersed with squeals of excitement as the frantic lizards dodged in all directions, finally making the fatal error of going underground, from where the girls dug them out and knocked them dead against a tree to take home. Sometimes when Susan or Jenny won a

A child's drawing of camp life after sundown.

reprieve for them, I took them to school and placed them in the disused aquarium which had been converted into a display case for desert wildlife. Other lizards lived behind our refrigerator, feasting on the insects attracted by the kerosene burner light. And one little family of white geckos slept all day in the ceiling and, as the evening shadows lengthened, they would creep out to wait in motionless ambush for unsuspecting moths.

I took one of the geckos to the fence one day and asked Billy for its Ngaanyatjarra name. He seemed rather disturbed that I was handling the creature and absolutely refused to touch it himself. He walked off and returned shortly with Noel who with his command of the more colourful aspects of the Australian language and gesture made it quite clear that men who handle geckos become impotent. Although not entirely accepting this theory, I did begin to treat the gecko with a little more caution.

I was keen to involve the class in an experimental method of learning that utilised their bush skills. A nature project seemed to be the most appropriate, and to prepare for it we began to collect mountain devils, or niari as they are more properly called. The niari looked fearsome with its armour of spikes, but in reality it was a delightful creature with the wonderful chameleon ability to change its colour to match its background. I chose them because they are so tough and leathery that they are rarely eaten by the Aborigines.

At the end of three weeks, we had ten of the diminutive lizards and the project was launched. On the back wall of the classroom I pinned a map of the mission area with a dispersal point marked with an X. Each niari was marked with an identifying blob of paint and that afternoon, after lunch, we walked the kilometre out to X and released all the lizards. We planned to wait one week then start to recover the niari, marking each recovery point on the classroom map. That was the plan but we hadn't taken into account an old camp woman who, returning from an unsuccessful fossick in the hills, had suddenly come upon an Eldorado of niari and promptly knocked the lot on the head and arrived home in triumph with spiny tails overflowing from her billy can.

One morning Andrea held out a small rusted tin. The lid had jagged edges suggesting it had been opened with a tomahawk. Shyly looking at her dusty feet she whispered, *'Tarkawara'*, I took the tin and cautiously peeped inside. A soft grey nose, long and whiskered, timidly snuffed at my fingers and retreated to the depths within.

'Tarkawara', Andrea repeated, plunged her brown fist into the tin and withdrew a cute little jumping marsupial mouse or Jerboa. A delightful gentle creature about twice the size of a city mouse, but with long pointed ears and a black brush at the tip of its dragging tail. The graceful legs were broken, the thin bones projecting through the fur.

'Why are the legs broken?' I asked.

She laughed at my concern and regarding me as a silly person, unwise in the ways of the bush, she answered simply, 'So they don't run away if we drop them'.

Joan brought in a marsupial mouse which gave birth to a litter soon after its arrival. However, a mystery soon surrounded the family as every day or so one of the tiny mice would disappear. Some of the class suspected me of trickery, others considered the unlikely possibility that the mother was eating her young. The mystery was solved when I came into the classroom one evening and saw a spider, the width of my palm, dragging a victim away. I immediately put a board over the cage to preserve the evidence and this became a terrific lesson on the following day.

The only creature in our growing classroom menagerie that gave us a few problems was a fledgling wedgetail eagle. When fully grown the eagle has a two metre wing span and can lift a small kangaroo off the ground. Carefully we released it into the large aviary we had outside the house, making quite sure that we kept clear of the claws and beak, that even in a young bird could rip the flesh from a hand. Mary called him 'Shylock' because he was always demanding his pound of flesh and had a voracious appetite that was rapidly depleting our meat reserves. One time he stuffed himself on the prime porterhouse steak we had air-freighted nine hundred kilometres from Kalgoorlie. Each day I threw a bag over Shylock and dragged him, squawks and all, into the school passage to give him flying practice. By the time he could negotiate the length of the passage he was already too dangerous to keep, for without warning he was likely to launch himself, talons foremost, at whoever was feeding him. One evening at sundown we took Shylock out to Brown Range and left him perched on a low branch of a dead tree and quietly walked away.

On another occasi— Andrea paused and pointed towards a stunted bush, and said, 'Little birds come out of their eggs.' So we wandered over and sure enough three finches lay huddled together, their soft round bellies completely naked of feathers. I was intrigued by her keen interest in birdlife and sensing my pleasure in the way that a sensitive child can, she took me to another four carefully hidden nests. In some, the eggs were unhatched. The reason for Andrea's interest was apparent a few days later when she and Ada came into the Mission swinging a closed-off jam tin billy packed with a mass of eggs and dead birds. Later as we strolled across to the shop, we saw them cooking these delicacies over a low fire.

During the daylight hours the desert children were the masters of their world. There were no secrets hidden from their ever-seeking gaze. They knew by the colour of the leaves of small stunted shrubs that a tempting fat white grub had infested the roots and they carefully dug the bush out with pointed sticks. One afternoon on a class excursion, I took part in this activity and soon had two white grubs about five centimetres long. I held them in the open palm of my hand.

'Can I eat them?' I asked.

'Yuo!' came the affirmative response, and I held the larvae head and chewed off the body as I had seen in movies. Then the children added a rider – '. . . but they make you sick if you don't cook 'im first.' I was still not asking questions the right way.

Every outing with the children was a lesson in basic survival and food gathering. They picked leaves from selected trees and small yellow berries from thin vines that hugged the ground and had, like everything else, a coating of dust. There was always something that could be eaten. There were other trees with red berries. I picked a handful of the inviting fruit.

'Can't eat 'im Sir', said Andrea and she deftly stripped a fistful from the slender branch and in the same action squashed them into a mushy red pulp, which she smeared over her face and arms.

'Very pretty?' Her laugh was a question.

On another occasion we were discussing woodcarving.

'Let's make little weapons', said Stanley, speaking for the boys.

'Good wood close-up', added Richard.

I wasn't going to be caught again by the 'close-up' routine, so I first of all made sure that this time close-up was only half a kilometre away. I still had memories of the close-up walk to Warapuya waterhole. But the enthusiasm was running hot and I didn't want to lose it in case the children withdrew into sullen hostility, so we decided to manufacture miniature weapons as a school activity.

In all Government primary schools in Western Australia, the girls were required to complete a program of sewing under the direction of a female teacher and during this same period the boys tackled a range of crafts under the general heading of 'manual'. So on the first day of Manual, the boys armed themselves with saws, knives and tomahawks and we headed into the bush. There were a few diversions along the way. On one occasion Richard detoured to show me a nest of ground birds. Carefully, he pointed out where the parent bird landed about seven metres

Neville Green with Mr Holland's family. A cluster of spears appear from the top of the wiltja.

away from the nest and then zig-zagged through the tufts of grass to take food to her young. To the Aboriginal children the tell-tale tracks led directly to a tasty dinner. Richard estimated that they would be ready to eat in a couple more weeks. I looked at the miniature fluff balls and doubted it. A lizard, the first of many, reared onto its hind legs and scurried through the scrub, vainly trying to keep a safe distance between itself and the children but within minutes it had been caught, killed and tucked under the belt of a senior boy.

When we reached the trees a squabble arose as several boys claimed the same elbow of wood for a boomerang. Finally a pecking order was invoked to decide the issue, and the youngest invariably lost. When everyone had four pieces of wood suitable to make a miniature boomerang (kali), a spear (nyintji), a woomera (miru) and a hitting stick (kupula), we set out on the return journey with all the tools loaded onto the two youngest boys, Fred and Ian. How they must have yearned to be older. Interest in this project ran high for just over a month and then I had to find something new.

My own education was not confined to the information imparted by the children, and I encouraged the men and women to visit me after school. When the store closed each morning the women and a few of the men commenced the daily quest for bush foods in the hills beyond the mission. They ambled out of the settlement, a few dogs loping beside them and several small naked children kicking up miniature dust storms in the rear. The babies were usually slung around their hips in cloth calicis, leaving their mother's hand free for the steel digging 'stick' and billy can. The calici, a recent innovation, was a sling of linen or calico worn diagonally across the body like a bandola and seemed to have been accepted by most of the young mothers. Before school finished, the women returned to take up their positions on the patch of grass near my front door, always with something new under the bent lids of rusting tins. As I approached them they beckoned with a backward toss of their head and pouted their lips towards the tins, and the contents would be revealed to the accompaniment of gleeful cries of 'Walkumun!' (good) and the supporting 'Yuo' (yes).

Each day my knowledge of the people and the desert environment grew and this was reflected in our classroom collection, which included minerals, meteorites, fossils, bones, seeds and a vast range of plant and insect life. Some became merely items of general interest while others triggered a series of lessons with a depth equal to any I had given in city schools.

JOSEPH'S DIARY

11 April
On Eeasther hoilday we went to old and put some on a then wee had drinc and went hunting then we caught a wild cat.

18 May
Lastnight Reggie was telling a story about a bodgie his name is Marlon Brando. One of man Who cannot smile.

4 November
Last night I was dreaming about that I was a indian that was rideing on a fastes horse in the world that night when I heard a noise of roster crow-rowing so I woke up and had a tea.

CHAPTER TEN
Further Days at School

Discipline was a problem related to cross cultural differences. Discipline in the school meant:

'Sit up straight!'

'Speak up!'

'Don't talk!'

'Look at me!'

'Don't look at me!'

It was a discipline invoked in the belief that it would develop concentration and produce industrious habits, which would result in improved reading, writing and arithmetic skills, and hasten the process of assimilation into Australian society.

Camp discipline had a different function. It meant that there were places women and children could not go; foods they could not eat; people near whom they could not be seen; demands of kinship, such as sharing, that had to be met. Yet in other ways the children experienced freedom to a degree unknown to the childhood of teachers and missionaries. If Mum swore at Fred, he swore back at her. If Dad threw a stick at Adrian for taking more than his share of the family damper Adrian retreated to a safe distance. The white adult's axiom of 'You'll catch it when you come home!' never seemed to apply in the Ngaanyatjarra family. When the child came home the matter was forgotten, providing the misbehaviour was neither of a sexual nature nor contravened a basic community value.

Discipline could be a problem at times, especially with the senior girls. In the past, the most disruptive element in the classroom had always been the girls closing ranks in solid opposition to the teacher. Boys, on the other hand, inclined towards individual and spontaneous misbehaviour, but they usually responded to reason, or in the extreme cases to physical force. In all dealings with Aboriginal children and adults, I observed one basic rule that saved me from the tremendous problems and actual violence that other teachers had known. I tried not to place anyone in a situation from which there was no withdrawal without loss of face. There had to be room for compromise. There was no place in the desert school for the autocratic 'do it now or else!' type of teacher. Both praise and reprimand were only effective if they did not isolate the child. This adjustment was usually difficult for a young teacher trained to reward individual achievement on the one hand and to identify and isolate troublesome children as a control technique on the other.

The white child gains great esteem by being asked to display his work to the class or by being praised before his peers. But when applied to a classroom of Aboriginal children it had a reverse effect, for not only did it cause immediate embarrassment but it provoked teasing in the playground. Praising a group of children lessened the embarrassment. A whispered word of pleasure to the child at the desk was acceptable and quiet praise when no-one else was present was also effective.

Similarly, the verbal rebuke that was a common control technique used by teachers may provoke unexpected anger and even violence. Forcing a Ngaanyatjarra boy to stand up for a misdemeanour caused him serious loss of face and younger boys and girls averted their eyes lest an unguarded glance be misconstrued and cause them to get a rock in the back during the next recess. The boy may regain face by a reprisal action against the teacher, which might be risky, or against the teacher's children, which was more common. During my first few weeks of teaching at Warburton, the punishments I meted out resulted in rulers, pencils and books being hurled across the room at my daughter, Susan, as soon as I turned towards the blackboard.

Lenny, after being growled at, stood sullen in the playground. His feet were agitatedly churning circles in the dust. He had a large rock in his hand. It would have been easy enough to rush him, to knock him to the ground, twist the rock out of his fist and drag him screaming and kicking into the classroom where he could decide whether to throw the glue bottle at me or at Susan. It had to be one of us or he would lose all respect in the eyes of the other children. Yet I found that it was always so much easier to adopt a firm tone and say, 'Wash your hands before you come in and don't be too long.' Then with everyone inside the school, Lenny began to feel a bit stupid standing outside on his own, so in exasperation he threw the rock at the toilet or onto the school roof, washed his hands and came inside to his seat. As far as I was concerned the discipline and the subject had ended outside; it was never broached again.

Richard, reprimanded, annoyed, and slouching in his desk was another example of the need for teacher tact. He was fourteen, two inches taller and ten kilos heavier than me. He stabbed the desk top with the point of an ugly looking pocket knife. His look was aggressive and challenging. The class was quiet, uncommonly quiet, their pencils held so lightly that they barely scratched the paper. No-one wanted to miss a word.

Fred sat two desks away from Richard. Poor 'Charley Brown' Fred.

'Awful work, Fred!', I adopted a stern manner. The class looked around at this turn of events. Richard paused in his tapping.

'Stand up, Fred! Show the class your pencil. See this silly boy writing with a blunt stick!'

Fred held up a pencil that was chewed and frayed.

'What must he do?'

'Sharpen it!' the class chorused, Richard and his threat was temporarily forgotten.

With mock anger, I berated Fred. '. . . and borrow that knife from Richard and sharpen it.'

Richard's sympathies were with Fred, so he gave him the knife and Fred loped down to the bin at the front of the class and managed to spread the shavings around the bin but not in it.

'Good boy, Fred! Nice and sharp! Now put the knife in the drawer of my table.'

Everyone knew I had won, but that was not the issue – no one had lost, and that was more important.

During the first two months, there were several incidents a week when angry parents intervened in child quarrels. A sudden lull in the playground noise immediately alerted us that a dangerous situation was developing. A woman might rush into the yard with a steel crow-bar or a handful of rocks, and there was no difficulty identifying the children who were involved. One would be crying in a high, carrying wail, while the culprit would be shuffling his feet in the dust, isolated from the others, for no one wanted to be near him when the rocks flew.

I soon learned that the first thing to do was to send the two children inside, for while the children remained in view the parents were obliged to maintain a show of anger. The next step was to invoke the 'Government property' rule and lead the man or woman outside the fence before listening patiently to their side of the story. That most of the speech was in Ngaanyatjarra was not important. The parent was getting it out of his system. Only once did I have trouble removing a parent. On one occasion Billy was adamant, and refused to accept my argument that, as the offending child was now inside, the matter was closed.

'No matter! I stay here all the time till she comes out again.'

'Come on, Billy,' I cajoled, 'bring those spears and sit outside the fence.'

'No!', he persisted, 'I bloody stay!'

He was determined to stay where he was until he had cracked a few skulls and in his present mood one might well be mine.

He stood there, almost two hundred centimetres in his bare feet, waving a mulga fighting stick above my head and shouting at the top of his voice. I didn't need to be fluent at Ngaanyatjarra to know that he wasn't very pleased at all.

With what calmness I could muster, I lifted my pack of cigarettes from my shirt pocket, put one between my lips and offered one to him. He immediately took it and demanded a light. In command of the situation again, I indicated that I would do so once we were outside the fence. As I walked off, he swore and followed. Reaching the fence I turned to light his cigarette but in his agitation he had already chewed it into a golden wad, so we sat in the shade of a tree and discussed the problems of children and swearing.

After that the school had two new rules. No adult Aborigines were permitted within the school grounds without my permission. The previous teacher had successfully prosecuted an aggressive parent so I could quote a

precedent to the men. And secondly, both children involved in
disturbances were to be punished. I felt at the time that it was the fairest
rationalization. Most of the playground disputes originated in teasing or
swearing. Joan told John that he had a twisted penis or something similar,
for the swearing was always of a derogatory sexual nature. John replied by
bouncing a rock off Joan's head. By punishing both, parental involvement
was avoided and the playground became a safe place for children. The
school punishment also prevented retaliation taking place at the camp and
forestalled a situation where men speared each other to vindicate honour.
The school could not be isolated from the community and conflict in one
had repercussions in the other.

In most schools, the principal makes up a list of school rules and
enforces them rigidly. I started with no rules and introduced them only
when a problem arose. New rules were explained so that everyone knew
the punishment for swearing, throwing rocks or being truant. In this way
the children came to accept the rudiments of law, with standardised
penalties that were not influenced by the emotional state of the Principal.
The children were not punished for anything that was not a rule that had
been previously discussed. There was a consistency to the system that the
children respected and their parents accepted. Although disciplinary
problems diminished, they did not disappear. Nevertheless parent
intervention in the playground became a rarity.

At recess the girls sat on the ground drawing patterns and figures
with sticks or bent wires as they exchanged stories and dodged the
occasional rocks thrown at them by boys who were bored. When they failed
to duck, there was frequently trouble in a big way. I was sure the problem
could be overcome if I could divert the aggressive energy into controlled or
directed activities. Playground equipment was almost non-existent. The
footballs and basketball I had brought to the mission had lasted three
weeks before the stony surface of the yard wore them out. The hand balls
had disappeared to camp and all but one of the cane hoops had long
before been cut up by the teachers to make punishment rods.

The Education Department would not make money available for
playground equipment – this was an area of parental responsibility – but
one thoughtful officer had suggested that I could either form a school
Parents and Citizens Association to raise funds, or alternatively ask the
parents to donate a few spears and boomerangs for sale in the city.
However, having been a voluntary worker with charitable organizations, I
realised that money could be obtained for worthy and impoverished
groups, Government schools excepted. The only way around the problem
seemed to be to tell most of the truth and no untruths, so my appeal
letters emphasised the mission, the traditional lifestyle and the need, but
made no reference to the school's Government status. In this way I
received a sizeable donation and immediately placed an order for
playground equipment which arrived on the truck in early May.

The day after the truck arrived, the boys set to work with crow-bars,
chipping away at the solid rock of the school yard to sink the equipment
into concrete. It took most of our free time for a week to get the holes

Warburton boys with new footballs.

completed and the concrete poured and set. I soon realised that it was not merely equipment being introduced but a new range of concepts.

A simple swing I had rigged up for my three-year-old daughter Tricia drew crowds of amazed children and adults who had never before seen a pendulum action and expected the child to continue on to disaster. But after several of the bolder children ventured onto it, the swing became a popular play activity for the junior children. This experience should have prepared me for the events that were to follow, but it didn't.

The first morning the new equipment was used it was bedlam. The excited children swarmed from the dining room and onto the bars, slides and swings. Few of the adults had seen the play equipment we take for granted and crowds of parents clutched the fence and gasped with horror as children climbed the steps and slid down the shiny steel of the slide. Only after we sent Tricia down the slide to prove it was safe did the fathers relax and drift away. During the day most of the camp people came to look and marvel. Our next problem arose a week later. The yells of about fifty stick-waving parents brought the teachers from the school. From behind the fence frantic mothers were throwing rocks at Richard and his crew. The giant stride, a modern maypole with steel loops on the ends of chains and a swivel top was the focus of angry attention. The senior boys had loaded the loops with the small boys and were rotating them at a speed that brought them almost horizontal to the ground. The unfortunate victims, reaching the limits of their endurance, were careening off in all directions. . . We had a new rule after that.

Although we could keep violence out of the school yard, it could not be checked on the mission or in the camp. One morning some young men gave cheek to a missionary. The missionary called upon a group of older men to reprimand the youths and in so doing inadvertently invoked tribal laws that demanded family loyalty in times of conflict. Within an hour, a relatively minor incident had snowballed into a full-scale tribal fight, as over two hundred men and women allied themselves with one faction or the other, joining in a melee of slashing sticks and jabbing spears. Many of the women still had their babies strapped to their backs, others dumped their infants into the declared neutral territory of the school ground for safety, grabbed fighting sticks and with shouts ran to the support of their families.

Tribal disputes carried over into the school, resulting in fights and angry words between the children. All were affected — some emotionally unsettled by the events, others anxiously listening to the sounds of raised voices to hear if their family was involved. The children's daily diaries, written each morning and accompanied by magnificent sketches, gave graphic accounts of camp life and the domestic issues that erupted almost on our doorstep.

One lunchtime our attention was drawn to an altercation between two men. The disturbance had arisen over senior school girls they were betrothed to. As the children came out of the dining room the two men took up duelling positions near the school fence. The children were ushered straight into the safety of the classroom. The men maintained a fast pacing parade for an hour and then returned to their camps.

This type of incident was not uncommon, because the girls stayed at school until they were fifteen and were able to communicate with teenage boys to an extent that had been forbidden under the old way of life. The girls liked this freedom and it was possible to see the beginnings of female emancipation. Permitting our own girls to roam with the Ngaanyatjarra girls also caused several minor revolutions against the ordered system.

One Saturday morning, my daughter Jennifer and a small group of girls were playing with dolls behind the wash shed when three boys about the same age came running towards them, shouting, yelling and throwing rocks. The girls instinctively jumped up ready to run but were held by Jenny's shout, 'Let's get 'em.'

The girls paused and then with whoops, grabbed up sticks and charged the boys, who were so flabbergasted at this unexpected turn that they were unable to believe what was taking place. It was real though, and Warburton was treated to the unusual sight of three boys being chased about the mission by a bevy of screaming girls.

But any such influence was temporary as Susan and Jenny were a minority group and soon came to feel the effects of majority cultural pressures. Within weeks of our arrival they began to pattern their behaviour to that of the Ngaanyatjarra girls and spent much of their leisure time in the playground playing knuckle jacks in the dust or hitting the ground with a story wire as they had seen the older girls doing. On weekends and after school they spent many hours in the company of the desert girls, exploring the creek beds, collecting wild onions, and joining in the excitement of lizard hunting. In the classroom the pressure to conform to the group norm caused them to set aside their personal desires for praise. They were visibly disturbed and even became resentful if I singled them out to display knowledge that would make them appear superior to the rest of the class. This was an unexpected turn of events. Before I arrived at Warburton, teachers had warned me that the Aboriginal children would not put up their hands, speak out in the classroom or answer questions. I was confident that they only needed a good model and within weeks the class would emulate Susan. I never expected the reverse effect.

It is invariably the members of the minority cultural group who are most seriously disadvantaged in the classroom. In outback Aboriginal schools, the children of teachers, missionaries and other white employees, suffer severe setbacks to their school work caused by peer pressures, by the *ad hoc* lessons of their teachers and by the sheer inability of parents and teachers to appreciate the stress upon the child who is endeavouring to maintain a balance between group norms and parental aspirations. These children often suffer additionally from the unconscious reverse racism of teachers who ignore the needs of the white child in order to maximise their success with the Aboriginal. When the two groups are compared, the Aboriginal child appears to have the greatest need and therefore demands the greatest allocation of time, but the needs of all children must be considered in equal measure. In the fringe towns where the inflow of Europeans overwhelmed the tribal population, the Aboriginal children became a minority group and were often culled off into special classes adjoining the school or segregated into groups within the classrooms where they barely survived from one year through to the next.

KEN'S DIARY

26 June
This morning as soon as the sun came up I was awak and when I went to my mothers camp I had damper and tea and I was the people fighting and I went towards Tommy Simms camp and I saw Howard and Roy Simms and my sister said you had your tea and damper and I said yes.

19 October
Last night when we was sleeping Donny Robinson said get up you boys we go and see the fight and I got up and ran. I thought they see devle but they said we going to see the fight and we came and see them and they finish the fight and we came back and went to sleep again.

CHAPTER ELEVEN

Visitors

I was in the store when I heard the news.

'The son of Lasseter is coming through soon', said Roy, looking over a stack of tinned meat balls and spaghetti.

'Yair? How did you hear this?'

'It came through on the radio that he was driving down from the Rawlinsons and to expect him.'

We chalked up our tins and, sliding back the door, stepped out where keen ears had picked up the message.

So Lasseter was coming; the name has a lot of magic in the inland. In the classroom I read the children excerpts from Idries' book *Lasseter's Last Ride* and pored over maps, pooling our knowledge, wondering just how close to the Warburtons Harold Lasseter had come in 1930. Stanley said there were old men down in the camp who had seen the fabled prospector during the final weeks before he died in the desert, in a futile attempt to rediscover a reef of gold that he had first seen more than forty years before.

On the last day of October, Bob Lasseter arrived. Rigged on top of the cabin of his landrover was a steel framed observation chair. Sitting in that chair he would be about as high as his father was on a camel. Bob Lasseter was a businessman, engineer and adventurer from New South Wales, on his second trip into this part of the country, searching for his father's reef of gold, and he enthralled the class with the story of his father's wanderings in the arid heart of Australia. But the children were at a loss to understand either the quest or the Wyalpula obsession for gold. Later in the day Joseph sketched Harold Lasseter standing beside a yellow nugget as large as a house. Below the picture was the brief caption: *Lasseter finds some gold.*

Whenever visitors arrived at the mission, I insisted that they came to the school. It was important that the children saw Wyalpula who were not missionaries or teachers. I wanted them to listen to the different patterns of speech, to learn about their work, their play and their homes. If the visitors were from abroad they pointed out their home country on a world map. At times I was doubtful whether the children could reconcile the narrow strip of blue on a map with the vastness of the Pacific Ocean, especially when they had never been to the coast. But they did understand that a person may live in one place but refer to another distant land as 'my country' for many of the children and their families were closely linked to tribal lands hundreds of kilometres away.

Foreign visitors who spoke in their native tongue amazed the children, as they had assumed that only Aborigines spoke anything but English. They roared with merriment as a Swiss geologist, Rudi, counted in French. Transferring to German he sparked a sudden and unexpected involvement of the children in a three-way language lesson.

'Head', I said, with my hand on Fred's head.

'Der Kopf', Rudi joined in.

'Kata', came the spontaneous response from the class.

'Nose!'

'Die Nase!'

'Mulya!' was the cry of total involvement and excitement.

The intensity continued in a rapid exchange of basic words and the children searched the classroom for new words to throw at Rudi. Through these visitors the children came to realize that there were other people who had to learn English, just as they did. With each new experience the world of the Warburton children stretched a little more.

Three tourists from the farming district of Wyalkatchem talked about wheat growing and sent a sample for the children to plant. These were the men who helped put flour in the mission store, but within the limited understanding of the desert children, flour was a substance that came on the truck from Leonora. It never occurred to them that it had not always existed in bags on trucks. As our grain crop ripened most of it disappeared into passing fingers, but even so we collected enough to grind into a coarse flour and prove that it was the same as that which the missionaries used for bread, and the Aborigines for damper. Wheat became a new word, and perhaps in a small way, a link between agriculture and food began to develop.

Small aircraft were arriving quite frequently towards the end of the year, and even the occasional helicopter no longer produced the stunned awe as when the first one arrived. Nevertheless, there were still events that brought the mission out in force. Such an occasion occurred when a DC3 carrying members of the Western Australian Ballet Company landed. Although it was a school day we all went down to the airstrip. The smaller children gasped as the Dakota circled over them before landing. It was the biggest thing most had ever seen and they were terrified by it.

When the introductions were completed, the passengers were invited to look over the mission and, of course, most of them wanted to visit the school, for children have a universal appeal, and these desert children were especially appealing.

We took the dancers to Rosemary's junior class. Shy, dark brown eyes watched every movement. As the ladies moved about the room, their slim hands were grasped by the youngsters, who fingered the texture of the white skin and puzzled over the painted nails and marvelled at the softness of the long hair. There was an emotional response from the dancers as the children sang nursery rhymes in the flat tones of a foreign and scarcely understood language. The visitors studied the writing and art of these six year olds. But it was the shy, almost furtive smiles that captured the hearts of the performers.

In David's room and mine the visitors could see the development wrought by dedication. A few children even whispered replies to the frequent questions. All the visitors were impressed and some quite emotional.

We followed the troupe back to the plane where they put on an impromptu ballet, hoping to inspire a corroboree from the Aboriginal men. They didn't have a hope! The city girls pirouetted daintily in stockinged feet, masking grimaces as they stubbed their toes on the rock strewn ground. While we were at the school with the troupe, some of the tourists who remained at the landing ground had been buying artefacts from the Aborigines. One enterprising young Ngaanyatjarra man even came up with an armful of artefacts that he had collected from the old men at the camp and was soon engaged in a brisk trade.

Only one incident marred a delightful visit. An avaricious woman, who dominated every discussion of Aboriginal customs, sighted Jimmy's beautifully carved woomera. Jimmy was a rare artist whose products demanded top prices. The old trade practice of 'Jackie gibbit boomerang – white fella gibbit baccy' was continually discouraged by missionaries and the Native Welfare Department. Striding up to Jimmy in her bombastic manner, she grasped the woomera, thrust a number of coins into his hand, and climbed straight on to the aircraft.

The passengers were aboard and the engines coughed into life when I noticed the puzzled look on Jimmy's face as he tried to sort out the value of the unfamiliar coins.

'Not much, Mr Green? Maybe?'

I checked the coins and could only agree.

'Yes, Jimmy, not much.'

There were twelve one-cent coins in his hand!

The children were keen observers of human behaviour, delighting in isolating a visitor's unusual expression or behaviour and converting it into an uproarious mime. I saw the possibilities of using this talent in the classroom, if only the children's shyness could be overcome. The day after the dancers left I noticed Melinda using a glove puppet to mimic the lilting steps of one of the dancers, so next weekend Mary made a range of glove puppets from old socks, cut up sheets, buttons, cottons and paints. A few pieces of timber and sheets of board provided the materials for a simple puppet theatre across one corner of the room. A loose bed sheet was hung down the front and concealed three children. Puppets proved a great success because they gave the children the opportunity to use their voices without the usual embarrassment caused by visual exposure. After a few weeks it was not uncommon for a child to disappear behind the screen and a few seconds later a bobbing puppet head would appear with an accompanying, 'Hey, you out there!', which was invariably followed by a volley of giggles. Much of the puppet talk was in Ngaanyatjarra and I could see by the sparkling glances in my direction and the smothered laughs, that my mannerisms occasionally became the subject of the puppet talks.

Concealing the child's physical presence was a simple device to develop free expression in the classroom and it was possible to extend this concept to other mediums, such as finger puppets made from match boxes, hand puppets from food packets and face masks painted onto paper bags and breakfast food cartons. While the enthusiasm for puppetry lasted, I directed it into role playing situations such as buying food at the store, using the Flying Doctor radio to explain an injury, describing a sickness to a nurse, and giving directions to tourists. At first the role playing was localised and focused on situations within the experiences of the community. Later I found it possible to move beyond the concrete to the hypothetical, as children, through role play, were encouraged to develop skills that may be essential if they moved to towns. They learned how to buy a ticket on a train, how to hail a bus, and the basic rules for crossing a road in town and driving a car in traffic.

I bought toy telephones and a new sphere of practical role play activities developed. Telephones produced an interesting spin-off in science and after I showed the class how sound could be conveyed between paper cups joined by string, 'telephones' became a popular playground activity; Joseph and Stanley even began an experiment to discover the optimal distance sound could be transmitted.

The relevance of telephones, trains and buses to desert children might be questioned. However, considering the changes in the lifestyle that were evident from the thirty years of mission contact, it was predictable that the adults would need more than local knowledge if they were to be able to respond confidently to the challenges that social and economic change would bring to their communities, or have any chance of survival if they ventured beyond the perimeters of a desert existence.

JAMES' DIARY

26 October
This morning when we came from the dening room I saw the plane coming towards the Mission and I said to Robert the plane his coming and he shout loud and said the airaplane his coming to land on the airstrip and all the children saw it come.

28 October
This morning Mr Green came in with the news and he told us a story about Lasseters son and Lasseter son came out looking for gold and later he found his fathers gold and he took it to over to Adelaide.

CHAPTER TWELVE

Language Teaching

We tend to think of a desert as a region of continuous heat, with searing winds that parch the land and destroy the body. It was something of a surprise to find that a winter's morning at Warburton could be bitterly cold. Chilling winds blew across the plain, and on such days the old people huddled within the warmth of the wiltja, while the children, knowing they must come up to the mission to eat, picked their way across the stony ground, the boys in the cast-off coats of city business men, the girls in desert stained dresses that may once have seen better days in the wardrobes of town ladies. When they came across to school, the girls huddled around tiny fires in saucepan shaped holes which protected the flames from the winds. These were fuelled with twigs from the girls' shade wiltja — for who needs a shade house in winter?

Inside the school it was not much warmer. The unlined aluminium walls and low roof seemed to convert the building into a giant freezer. The floor was bare, unfriendly concrete, and the children withdrew their feet from the chill underneath and most knelt on their chairs. Someone in the Education Department must have been sympathetic to the situation, for the school had been allocated a regulation wood box for each of the three classrooms, and these items were to be dutifully shown on the principal's annual inventory of school furniture. The fact that there were no stoves or fireplaces in the school had not occurred to the stores clerk in Perth. When I completed the annual inventory I added a memo that termites had eaten the boxes during the summer vacation, and ended one administrative chore.

'Apple! Apple! Andrew! Andrew!' Daily the chant penetrated through the thin walls. Daily the list of words in the middle classroom was hammered onto the children's memory — and mine.

'How else but by rote learning?' David asked. 'They must acquire a basic English vocabulary before they can even begin to read or speak.' This was not an uncommon response — for many teachers, then and now, rely heavily on rote learning.

Language was a continual problem. English was only used within the classroom. Beyond this, it was a world of dialect. A migrant child new to Australia finds he is surrounded by English. In shop windows, in comics, at school, on radio and television, he meets a steady stream of the new

Classroom charts for a bilingual programme.

language and consequently his learning rate in English is accelerated. But this is not the case with the Aboriginal child in a desert school. Exposure to English is not enough, for the teacher must understand the special distinctions of the child's home language.

The Ngaanyatjarra dialect has sounds for which there are no English equivalents and Aboriginal adults were continually correcting my faulty speech as I tried to express sounds that exist mid-way between 't' and 'd'; 'k' and 'g'; 'p' and 'b'.

There was an appalling lack of understanding of the Aboriginal child's struggle to speak standard English. Education administrators rarely visited the remote Aboriginal schools and even those who knew the situation gave only lip service to the language problems of the Aboriginal child.

We obtained hundreds of magazines from friends in Perth, and we made these available to the children to read at school and sometimes take home. There was always a pile of comics and magazines on our verandah for the men and women who wanted to sit and read, or maybe just glance at pictures of another world. Peeping unseen through the glass louvres of our loungeroom, I saw an old man look longingly at a full paged colour advertisement of tinned fruit. He furtively glanced around to be sure that he was unobserved and then swiftly scooped his fingers over the pictures with accompanying sounds of epicurian delight.

The introductory reading books provided by the Education Department for Aboriginal children were accepted in most Western

Australian schools. In common with primers of the day, the books were written around an urban middle-class family with the inevitable dog, cat, baby and ball. The middle-class language of the readers was just as irrelevant as everything else in text books and the words in the introductory book made this scheme quite impractical for desert children. The Anglo-Australian child looked at page two and said, 'Here is Fluff', but the Ngaanyatjarra children, whose language has no sounds for 'h', 's' or 'f' could only, at the best, produce a sentence, "ere ei Plupp'.

The purchase of an alternative reader was out of the question on our meagre three dollars per year per child allowance, so the teachers in the junior classes tried to compensate by introducing local word lists that could be placed on charts and learned by rote. A previous principal had obtained twenty sets of *Bush Books*, a series of books with Central Australian Aboriginal themes of hunting and gathering. These were popular and well used. But with everything unorthodox that we tried in the Aboriginal classroom there was a nagging concern that when the District Superintendent of Education arrived, we might be called to account and be found lacking.

I never envied Rosemary and David in the formidable task they had in developing English skills in these young children. By the time the children came into the senior classroom they had five years of conscientious teaching behind them. Yet they still did not have sufficient control of English to be able to organize a coherent sentence. Most had mastered the skill of copying words from the blackboard, so their work books gave the illusion of literacy. Eventually I resorted to a technique I had used with remedial children; every sentence was broken into three parts — when, who and what, and the children were encouraged to write about their home experiences. The first lesson of the day was Daily Diaries and these began, not with words, but with pictures, for in detailing the pictures the children were leisurely translating the components into English. When the picture was well under way the story began to flow into the three parts. At first they gave only a single, uncertain sentence, but before the end of the year the older children, such as Stanley and Melinda, were putting together exciting stories about camp life.

One day Billy, sitting by the tank, looked up suddenly with a cry of 'Truck! Hoi!' He stood up abruptly to study the wisp of dust in the distance.

The old people in the shade of the hospital trees stirred from their position near the dripping tap and prodded the dogs with sticks. The young men sitting on the store verandah laughed with the eternal delight of youth, stretched their legs and rose, slapping the dust from their trousers, to shout the news. Down at the camps, the young women who had been poking sticks at the fires while they gossiped, now slung their babies on their hips and headed in the direction of the mission. All feet moved towards the gate — all eyes watched the puff of dust rising above the gate beyond the creek.

A kilometre down the road the blue truck emerged from the shadows of the creek gums, picking up a running escort of children as it approached the mission gate. Slowly it moved past the waving crowd until it turned the corner to halt outside the Superintendent's house. As the dust-covered driver stepped down from the cabin he tossed out the mail-bag, our first letters for six weeks.

I was always searching for ways to stimulate the children to respond to formal learning and one of the most successful ventures began by chance.

The arrival of the mission truck was a great occasion. Every three to six weeks the truck made the run from Leonora, loaded with supplies, mail and, occasionally, with Aborigines sitting on top. Because it was a special occasion, the entire class would break to go outdoors to witness the arrival and to pick up news of relatives. When Mary brought our mail over, she sat in the classroom eagerly telling me the news of family and friends. I suddenly looked up and realised that Stanley, Joseph and other seniors were watching us closely.

'How many of you kids have ever had a letter?' I enquired.

Cora partly raised her hand — sufficient to attract my attention.

'Who from?'

'Sister', she whispered.

Some relied on missionaries to draft out the few letters they sent. I had the germ of an idea and my next question was intended to sound out the potential.

'Who has relatives at Laverton or Mt Margaret?'

Nearly every hand went up; so we talked about letters and everyone wrote out a list of all the people they could write to. We had no money for stamps but we could use the occasional travellers and government officers as couriers to take out letters to distant towns and settlements.

'Would you like to write a letter to a relative or friend at Laverton?'

The response was lukewarm, for writing in English was not easy, and sending letters didn't seem much like fun. That afternoon the children learnt how to write letters. They began to ask questions — 'What do we write?' 'How do you spell . . . .' School education was beginning to have some relevance and the enthusiasm grew.

The letters were bundled up and sent to the Principal of Laverton school along with my earnest appeal for a reciprocal batch of letters by the next government courier.

Three weeks later, we got our first replies. The Native Welfare projects officer dropped them off on his way through to the border. I had sent the Laverton Principal a list of all the names in my class so each child, even my daughter, had a letter. It was a great beginning.

The children were guaranteed privacy and their letters were not corrected or censored. If children wanted to know a word — it was whispered. I think half of the teacher's communication in a desert school is done at a whisper level. We also developed a list of frequently used words that were charted for convenience. When the letters were completed the children sealed the envelopes to ensure privacy. By mid-year letters from older brothers and sisters who had left school were added to the courier bag — and the Laverton and Warburton schools became centres for the community mail service.

Letter writing was never regarded as a lesson and if there was a lull in the classroom routine and I put the question —

'What would you like to do?' the class would respond in one voice — 'Letters!'

I was still learning that all school work can be interesting to children — if the teacher can demonstrate its relevance in such a way that the child no longer sees learning as a chore but as a pleasure, with something in it for himself.

ADA'S DIARY

3 October
On Saturday morning we went for a walk to the old well and then we gone to get water in the billy can and we caught a lot of goanna, niari and bobtail and we be getting lots of wild honey and we came back to the old well.

13 October
Last night when we were all sitting near the big fire, Edgar said listen all the men fight over there far away but we nearly went to see, but we was too cold and we stay near the fire.

20 October
This morning Ivy, Kathrom, Roma and I were playing marbles with Quandongs seeds. Suddenly I turn around and listen. We heard the plane come to Warburton.

CHAPTER THIRTEEN
Books and Movies

As our wheat crop began to form heads of grain, I decided to relate the milling process to a familiar activity and offered to exchange a cup of dry tea and sugar for a cup of spinifex seed. The next afternoon Billy and his three wives were waiting at my door. We transferred the classroom to the front of the house, and my lessons began to a chorus of laughter from the children and good humoured advice from the women. Twenty minutes later, despite skinned knuckles, I had enough flour to make one small damper, which I cooked on the kitchen stove. Quite proud of my achievement I took it out to be sampled by my audience.

'Not as good as bush damper in the camp', was the frank reply. 'Bush damper big!' and just how big Billy indicated with the spread of his hands. I found this hard to believe until two nights later the secret was revealed. A 'hoi' at the fence brought me out to Billy, who held out an empty tin with the request for baking powder for his wives to mix into the damper flour.

On long weekends and public holidays, the mission dining room was closed. If the parents failed to hunt or gather, there was no food for their children, who were then forced to scavenge in the rubbish bins of the white staff.

The children knew that the whites maintained a regular schedule of meal times and they also knew when each household dumped their kitchen scraps into the two hundred litre petrol drums that served as rubbish bins. The dogs also knew. Each day resolved into a battle of wits between hungry children and starving dogs. When the bins were almost empty it needed two children to work together — one to hold the legs of the other and prevent the forager falling amongst the bottles, tins and burnt refuse in the depths of the bins. At the slightest hint of a door opening, they quickly scampered off to one side of the bin with a pretence of just arriving. If it was a missionary they would say, 'Church day tomorra?'; if a teacher, 'School tomorra?'

At Warburton we constantly tried to give the children new insights into the outside world. Pupils at a city school spent months collecting pictures which they sent to Warburton. Consequently the entire rear wall of the classroom was a kaleidoscope of colour, depicting life in many parts of the world. From a range of over a thousand pictures, Betty, Stanley and the senior group altered the display at will throughout the year.

The Warburton Wyalpula community represented only a narrow cross-section of Australian society. Teachers and missionaries were not the sort of people the Ngaanyatjarra would meet in the towns and, although it was impossible for me to take the children to the world, it was possible to bring the world to them through films, tapes, radio and records, and that is what I endeavoured to do. The children spent hours of free time looking at, talking over and asking about different aspects of life in other places; comparing ethnic groups, looking at homes and animals, both familiar and strange. Through pictures, a transfusion of knowledge about the world beyond began to take effect. Pictures of black people sparked great interest and *Life* magazine coverage of the Los Angeles riots was keenly discussed by the older boys and the subject must have continued at camp, as some of the young men stopped by to borrow the magazine and asked me to explain the story beyond the pictures.

Also, the entire desert region was coming under the scrutiny of large oil and mining exploration companies and Hunt Oil was drilling only eighty kilometres from the mission. One weekend the school and mission staff were invited out to the Hunt oil rig and I managed to borrow a movie that had been flown in to entertain the crew. Two nights later, Warburton had its first full length, non-religious film, when Gregory Peck as Captain Horatio Hornblower flashed his sword across the silver screen, which was only one of our double bed sheets stretched between two poles in the school yard.

Most of the adults sat on chairs from the classrooms, while at the back, a few of the older camp people clustered, their long slim spears silhouetted against the skyline, while the children hunched close to the screen.

The rough conditions didn't dampen the enthusiasm of the audience, and there were requests for a replay the following night. On the second night, a dozen sticks challenged the swords of the villains. One miniature spear transfixed a pirate to a chorus of cheers, which turned to riotous laughter when the scene change showed the spear hanging over the heroine's ear. In a sense it was reminiscent of the Saturday afternoon movie matinees of my own childhood, when all the neighbourhood boys went to the cinema armed with cap guns and rubber daggers to harass the screen villains.

During the next week, dozens of makeshift swords were confiscated from the boys in the playground and the whole pattern of child play was radically changed as ships, forts and boarding parties materialised. As the year advanced, movies were shown every week and had a marked influence on the thought, art and play of the children. Aboriginal men were no longer sketched barefooted, but with high heeled boots, and occasionally a neckerchief and stetson. It was sometimes a little disconcerting to see an Arizona cactus materialise in an Australian desert landscape. Cowboys and Indians dominated the general conversation and movie catalogues were read avidly.

On picture nights the children did not return to camp after tea. The girls sat on the ground under the trees and told stories in the dust, while the boys climbed on the tankstand, queued up with flat boards to slide down the pile of mullock behind the school or impishly threw rocks at the girls. On clear nights, Stanley and Richard helped tie up the bed sheet and bring a desk from the classroom to serve as a table for the 16mm projector.

'Ring the bell?' It was a demand and question in one, the way Andrea said it.

At my nod, there was a general stampede to grab the spot right under the screen, where the baddie could be stabbed with a spear before his gun was halfway out.

Later in the year, a mining company established a base camp near Warburton and offered to erect a steel framed screen. This was opposed by the mission, so I offered the school grounds for a screen and the use of the projector if the company paid for the films and flew them in. The selection of films was left to a combined committee of the government and mining staff, with several of the Aboriginal men occasionally attending. The film catalogues became the most important reading material in the classroom, and sparked questions about the pronunciation of names. There was great delight when movie stars were found to have the same names as some of the class group.

Nine years later I revisited Warburton and was pleased to find that Stanley had established himself as a travelling movie man, taking his projector and hired films to the outcamps to show movies at two dollars a head.

ADRIAN'S DIARY

3 November
Last night when I was going to my mother's camp suddenly I saw to horses coming to drink the water and I ran a way and I saw Livingston and Benjemen coming and I told them the horses are coming lits go and see. And I didn't went to see my mother becuese I was looking at the horse.

10 November
Tomorrow will be pictures and it's about Jams Stuart we might see him shooting and he'll win and get's his gun and all the people might shout. when he win's it and other cowboys were wild because he win that gun.

CHAPTER FOURTEEN
The Measles Epidemic

In July, we were given government approval to take a team of children to the district sports carnival at Laverton, five hundred kilometres away. In the past, the road had been considered too dangerous and, only the year before, a government truck had rolled over on a bad section. The Native Welfare and the mission offered to provide transport while the missionaries at Mt Margaret were willing to bed down the children. This was to be the first team to represent Warburton Ranges at a district sports carnival.

The children became highly competitive for the limited places in the school team, not for the joy of competition but because it was an opportunity to visit relatives in the town, press noses against the grubby glass of a real store window and go to a movie theatre. Sports preparation began in earnest and children on their way to school trained up and down the kilometre length of airstrip. Hours of puffing and sweating went into digging and carting river sand for the long jump pit. Everywhere there were children running. The girls, showing the effects of the mission emphasis on modesty, ran awkwardly as they tried to hold their long dresses below their knees.

We ordered documentary films from Perth about the Olympic Games and the children studied the style of the champions. The American negro athletes attracted special attention as the children seemed to identify more readily with blacks — and cheered the events won by black athletes.

A great sportsman once said that even if you are not the best cricketer in the world you can look like one and we were determined that our team would look like winners. Mary and the mission women made the girls' sports tunics in royal blue with gold sashes. Rosemary spent hours sewing a school flag in blue and gold with a leaping golden kangaroo. On the Warburton school sports day the flag was given a public viewing as it unfurled from a sturdy two metre spear made by one of the fathers.

Sports day had once had special significance for the population of Warburton. In the early years it was held on the last day of the school year and was followed by the break-up dinner. After that, the children and their families departed to the windmills and favourite camp sites far from the mission. On those occasions, a beef steer had been slaughtered and given to the people. One year a bullock fell down the well and the mission

The athletics team ready for the inter-school carnival.

generously doubled the handout; the drowned beast plus another for hauling it out of the missionaries' drinking water. But those sports events had been held in the searing heat of summer. In more recent years they had been transferred to the cooler months of winter.

As a prelude to our final selection, a school sports day was organised and race lanes were marked out on the airstrip. The school captains marched their teams to the area where the whole camp population attended. We tried unsuccessfully to get parents to participate, and only the Wyalpula community assisted with the marshalling, recording, and other duties of the occasion. It was a great day, and the fact that some children ran the wrong way and others refused to budge from the starting line didn't seem to matter to anyone.

With the teams selected, and the uniforms completed, it seemed that nothing could upset the long awaited trip. Then, one night, a family recently returned to the mission came to the hospital with a sick child. After a hasty radio consultation with the Flying Doctor, the nurses' worst fears were confirmed and a measles epidemic, one of the most dreaded scourges of Aboriginal society since the arrival of Europeans, was about to explode upon the desert outpost.

Australian parents accept the likelihood of their children catching measles and it no longer causes very much concern, because generations of contact had tended to lessen the effects. However, the Aboriginals of Australia have no such immunity against minor European ailments and the effects of these diseases can be devastating and tragic. As soon as measles was confirmed at Warburton, the doctor radiod that he would fly in.

The children watched the blue Beechcraft of the Flying Doctor glide down for a landing. Apprehensive eyes followed the twin rows of dust that rose in spiral puffs from the hard black wheels. Would someone be taken away and never come back? That was the question in many minds. Most of the illnesses were capably handled at the hospital and the daily radio schedule kept the doctor in touch with his patients, even though they were nearly a thousand kilometres apart. His arrival usually meant that someone was seriously ill. Through fear and innocence many patients were kept in the bush by relatives until their condition was critical, consequently many of those flown to hospital were too sick to survive and never returned. It was hardly surprising that the Aboriginal people of the desert came to regard the blue planes as the agents of death, rather than the couriers of life.

The deaths of people who were flown out was one concern, but there was also the matter of the dead being buried in pauper graves in town cemeteries. Burial was part of a Dreaming cycle which included conception, birth, manhood, parenthood and death. Unless the correct burial ceremonies were completed the spirit could not be freed to await reincarnation and the cycle would be destroyed.

There was always tribal concern for the dead who were not buried according to the laws and rites of the Ngaanyatjarra, a concern that was scarcely understood and rarely considered by white doctors and officials. We place great emphasis on our burial procedure and ceremony, and consider it of prime importance that we know where dead relatives are interred, yet many Aborigines are removed from their country and buried in lonely, unmarked graves in alien town cemeteries that are unknown to their families.

Daily the measles contagion spread and entire families dragged themselves to the hospital grounds, where they lay in the dust, oblivious to the pain, the flies and the dogs. The school numbers dwindled and halved. Over the mission hung a pervading sense of fear and misery and not one family was left unaffected by the epidemic.

Several times the Flying Doctor was summoned to serious cases. Sometimes he arrived too late and the mourning wails of the relatives conveyed the tragic news to the camp. To keep the disease from spreading to any other Aboriginal community, the doctor quarantined the mission and placed a ban on movement to or from the settlement. Consequently the sports trip had to be cancelled.

At the time of the measles epidemic, the hospital huts and grounds were packed with the sprawled bodies of the sick. The children, some lying on old jute sacks but most with only the dirt beneath them, shivered and sweated. Alongside each patient, to be shared with the dogs and flies, were small meat tins of medicine and water. How different from the well tended white children tucked between clean, ironed sheets. I hunched down beside Andrea and softly called to her. The dusky lids of her eyes opened, but the face was too wracked with illness to move. I brushed dust from the hand that lay clenched in the dust and stood up, wondering about the progress man had made in medical science.

That week the first child died. A sound in the night awoke us. An eerie cry, long and outdrawn, like that of an animal in pain. We lay in the darkness listening as other voices took up the cry, relaying it to the camp. Outside the hospital fence the family gathered to wail away the night until sunrise. Each wail was held on its monotone note, strengthened and renewed by the group in a rising, falling, unending cry.

Three weeks later the mission was back to its normal routine, but in the classroom the impact of the disease was more lasting. The children were subdued, drained of the vitality they normally displayed during the mid-year months. The sparkle had gone, the classroom rapport was difficult to recapture and we regressed to a dull routine as the teacher and pupils ritually acted out their roles.

RICHARD'S DIARY

3 November
Yesterday after tea we and some boys and Jackie said will we playing crooks and cowboys and Jackie said yes we play where that old house and I said yes and we ran to the shed.

9 November
I saw Ivan and Ricky looking at the Phantom book upside down and I looked and I said your too little go home and I took the book off the two boys and they went home and I sat down. I was looking at the pictures and reading the word.

CHAPTER FIFTEEN
New Knowledge and the Old

When a person is buried according to custom, the spirit is released to await re-birth in another Ngaanyatjarra child. Some of these spirits were mischievous and visited their living kinsfolk through dreams. Others lingered near the wiltjas in which they previously lived. They were very active after dark and were believed to be carnivorous.

On film evenings, I set up a pilot light in the school yard to be switched on while the reels were changed, for on several occasions the sudden gloom had brought on a nervous muttering amongst the crowd. 'Mamus' was furtively whispered between lowered heads as a family hastily gathered up their blankets, babies, and dogs and hurried back to camp; the children clinging close to the parents. The rest of the audience watched the film with increasing anxiety, each with a personal fear of being left alone in the darkness, where they would be an easy prey to the spirits. Then suddenly they would all depart leaving only the upturned chairs and a haze of dust drifting across the beam of light bridging the emptiness to the screen.

About mid-year, the school dentist was due, so it was an opportune time for a lesson on teeth. The senior children were sent home with instructions to scour the campsite and the surrounding bush for teeth and jaw bones. The following morning all the exhibits were placed in a box at the front of the class. Amongst the children's collection I slipped a whale's tooth I had collected years before when I visited a coastal whaling station.

As each tooth was held up the class delighted in displaying their bushcraft. Exclamations in Ngaanyatjarra and English were excitedly bandied about the room as all, from the oldest down to little Fred, vied to show off their knowledge of the haunts and habits of the local animals.

"Who found this?" I asked, picking out a jaw bone with several teeth intact.

Stanley's hand went up and he shyly commented on it, explaining to me that it was the jaw of old Billy's dog, that the teeth were pointed for meat eating and killing, and that the dog had been accidentally killed while trying to steal a freshly baked damper. The old man had been very sad, for the dog had been a good hunter.

All this was very ordinary to bush children, but suddenly they caught my puzzled expression as I looked into the depths of the box.

'This is a different one!' My tone was one of surprise and I suddenly held up the fifteen centimetre whale's tooth.

The silence was sudden and prolonged, broken only by a rapidly expelled 'Ha!' — the Ngaanyatjarra expression of surprise.

'Who brought this in?' I asked, moving about the class.

No reply.

'What is it then?' A moment of thought.

'Mamu', suggested Richard, and at once a dozen heads nodded in agreement.

'What's a mamu?' I pleaded ignorance, hoping for some clue of the desert child's innermost beliefs; beliefs which they had learned to hide from the scorn and laughter of the white men.

'Big thing!'

'Ghost!'

'Devil with teeth!'

The voices were hushed and cautious.

'I think I saw one the other night as I walked down to the creek.'

A sudden rustle of interest. The missionaries had always ridiculed the idea, yet here was a Wyalpula who was not only interested but may also have seen a mamu.

'Has anyone here seen a mamu?' I cautiously asked.

A volley of hands shot into the air and everyone was shouting at once. It was a sudden childish burst of eagerness to talk about this taboo subject. It was an enthusiasm that makes a teacher know that he is communicating.

The period that followed was one of those rare and incredibly beautiful moments in a teacher's career, a fragment of time when the social wall that separates the wonderful and imaginative world of children from the realism of adulthood disappears, and there is sincere, respecting and responsive communication.

'Perhaps someone could draw a mamu for me and I could see if that was what I saw.' I was musing aloud to the class. Colours and paper came out with a deafening clamour and then there was a busy silence as the children, perhaps for the first time, tried to transfer their inner fears onto paper. They now expressed these fears in a form that had never been influenced by the comic book ghosts and science fiction monsters of television that stereotype the art of the town child. The results were incredibly simple and no two were the same. Teeth, painted and large, were quite conspicuous and a few creatures reflected the mission teaching by possessing a pointed tail and horns. For a while we talked softly about mamus then put the papers away to return to mundane matters.

One of the most exciting teaching experiences was the discovery that the Ngaanyatjarra children were enthusiastic stargazers and that the sky, stars and planets feature in the Dreaming stories, many of which emphasise Aboriginal values and describe the punishment of those who disregard tribal laws. The people of Warburton slept out on the ground, under a canopy of the brightest stars to be seen anywhere in the world — under a sky that for ninety nights out of every hundred is clear and still. Parents knew this sky and used it like a picture book to teach the sky lore of the Dreaming.

One story tells how Yula was travelling across the land in the Dreamtime carrying a most sacred object when he saw seven women ahead of him. He was almost upon them when they turned and seeing him, fled. For many days, Yula pursued the women but they eluded him. Eventually he trapped them at a waterhole in a blind gorge.

When his advances were resisted he promised to exchange the secrets of the sacred object he carried in return for the women's company. But, before the bargain could be sealed, the Great Snake Spirit of the waterhole, angered by this evil conspiracy, hurled first Yula, then the women, into the blackest part of the sky, to remain there as an eternal warning. Yula became the giant star Betelgeuse; the women, the seven stars of the Pleiades. The people of the desert told me that if you lie outside at night and watch the stars drift across the sky, you can see Yula high above, still trying to catch the same women he pursued in the Dreamtime.

Astronomy also had a practical application in the desert culture. Some ten thousand years ago, showers of glossy black meteorites fell across parts of the North American continent, South East Asia and Southern Australia. Only in the arid desert areas of Australia are these still found on the surface. American scientists studied them to devise a space capsule that would survive the re-entry into the earth's atmosphere and gem collectors polished them to expose their jet sheen. But long before Europeans discovered them, Aboriginal doctors were using these meteorites as part of their healing kit. When I showed an interest in these, the children and parents brought in dozens. About the same time I received a magazine article that described how they originated from the impact of a meteorite on the moon's surface thousands of years before. The article excited a lot of interest in meteorites, satellites and space exploration.

The year before, the children had seen the horizon light up as the magnificent Seki comet spread across a third of the night sky. Now they watched for shooting meteorites and they plotted the course of a dozen satellites that crossed overhead. Each morning we followed these observations in the classroom by referring to newspaper reports, articles and books. Quickly they added new stories to their evening star watching, distinguishing American weather satellites from Russian Sputniks and manned orbits. So too they learned to identify planets and recognise constellations. There developed the dual blending of Western and Aboriginal culture. All children knew where to find the Great Hunting Eagle in the heavens. Their delight was wonderful when they realised that it was also the Southern Cross of their Australian Flag and as they added in the eagle's hitting stick we discovered together the names Alpha and Beta Centauri, the pointers for the cross.

Our first formal study required nightly observations of the phases of the moon which were sketched the following day. From the first sliver of a new moon to the blazing glory of the full moon rising, each child maintained a diagrammatic record of its nightly changes. It was a simple activity, but one which introduced Ngaanyatjarra children to the basic principles of the scientific studies of observation, recording and prediction.

It is difficult for city people to appreciate the brilliance and the closeness of the desert sky at night time. One night several members of a geological team were having a meal out of doors as guests of the mission, when a glow beyond the trees caused them to exclaim, 'My God! Our camp's on fire!'

They rushed to the vehicles and drove like fury towards their caravan camp, but half-way there, sheepishly returned to the party with the golden desert moon rising behind them.

After the moon study, I found the children wanted to learn more about European ideas of stars, so for the next few weeks we searched the night sky for the planets of our solar system. At the time Venus was easy to find, because it was low on the horizon and produced weird illusions as it appeared to bob about.

One night in October, a strange object appeared in the sky above the mission. It was a large moving point of light, cone-shaped like an inverted parachute – quite a puzzle. Obviously a Wyalpula could explain it. But the Wyalpula on the mission couldn't and the camp soon erupted in chaos. The women clutched at the smallest children and huddled within the wiltjas. The men grasped handfuls of sand which they hurled into the air with screams, curses and pleadings, many voices mingled in an incoherent roar. From one of the camps a flurry of spears was launched into the sky, they lifted, held a moment, and their energy spent, crashed with a dry rattle among the rocks.

In the classroom next morning, I feigned ignorance of the strange light in the sky and the whole class eagerly took out paper and pencils to recreate the scenes of the previous night, and write their own explanations. Most suggested that it had been a satellite; others who remembered the magnificent Seki Comet of the previous year, reckoned it was a comet. Two saw it as a sign from God, and one boy thought it was a ghost. Education was already beginning to over-ride the traditional beliefs of the older generations. The children were beginning to look for scientific explanations. How long would it be before they began to question the stories of the Dreaming, upon which their tribal religion was based?

STANLEY'S DIARY

15 April
Last night I saw some boys sitting round the fire. They were singing some cowboy songs.

9 May
This morning I saw some men fighting in the camp. One man was speared through the leg and he had to come up to the hospital.

9 May
Last week I was play spear fight with Jeff. He got one and speared me on the leg.

19 May
Over the holiday Ben, Bert and I went hunting along the way we shot one turkey. It was a fat one. Bens father said your a good boy.

27 October
Last night when we were sitting outside the tent and we heard some of the men shouting. They were saying look up in the sky it was in the west and I looked up it was moving. It was like a comet but it were bright and yellow and it was moving toward the moon. I think it was a rocket.

CHAPTER SIXTEEN
Tribal Education

When someone died, the living area in the vicinity of the deceased's hut was immediately vacated to avoid the 'mamu spirits' that lingered in the air to devour intruders. Within weeks all usable sheets of iron and pots from the abandoned area were transferred to the new camp site.

A death at camp always affected the behaviour of children at school. Apart from the emotional disturbances stemming from the loss of relatives, there were other important customs. The names of the dead were never spoken and people of similar name were called Kunmunura which means 'no name'. When old Queenie died, our singing of the National Anthem at morning assembly became rather ragged, with blanks of stubborn silence where the word 'Queen' should have been.

The death of Norman earlier in the year left its mark on the school library, as the senior boys methodically blotted out every reference to Norman that occurred in the small collection of books. The story of Robin Hood with its frequent references to the Norman knights was given special attention.

On another occasion I called on a boy to demonstrate a lesson point at the blackboard.

'Albert,' I said, offering him the chalk, 'come out to the front please.'

No reaction.

'You, Albert!', louder this time as I pointed right at him. 'Out the front!'

Stanley interrupted. 'That's Tom, Sir — a new name.'

That stopped me. Then it was suddenly obvious. Old Albert had died in the camp — and with him his name.

'Okay, Tom. Come here!' And Tom, ex-Albert, smiled and ambled out. The class relaxed as a tense situation was averted. Sir was learning quickly; for a Wyalpula.

Joseph and Stanley hung back after school and I could sense they had something important to say.

'You like to come to boys singing, Sir? Dennis and Bobby said to ask you.'

'When?', I responded with the right amount of eagerness. I was very keen, for I knew that for several weeks past the Bush boys had been holding regular song sessions.

'Tonight. Some of the boys come up here when it's almost dark and take you there . . .', they hesitated. I knew there was more to come.

'Smokes?' It was a question that was made more emphatic by pointing two fingers to his nose.

I nodded assent with a 'Yuo!'

Payment in food and cigarettes was an accepted obligation for those invited to attend an adult ceremony. In this case they were all boys but still the courtesies applied.

Dennis, Bobby and James were three Bush boys, or novices, who had been sent out of the camp by the elders; to the women of their families the boys were symbolically dead until re-incarnated as men through initiation and circumcision. In the traditional days, they would have had to fend for themselves for periods of up to a year. But the sedentary mission life had wrought many changes to the traditional customs, for during the daylight hours the boys wandered in the bush beyond the mission, taking care that they kept out of the sight of forbidden relatives. To make sure that they obeyed the tribal laws, several men kept a vigilant eye upon them. At sundown the boys came in close to the mission to a pre-arranged point and uncles or friends took them food.

This was a period of discipline and the novices were often subjected to outrageous teasing by those men permitted to visit and instruct them in the tribal law. They might be denied cigarettes and tobacco for several days and then an uncle or friend would greet them, tossing a tobacco tin and cigarette papers on the ground at their feet. For hours the men would sit, smoke, talk and instruct while the tobacco tin remained unopened and the novice impatiently anticipated the pleasure of a cigarette, unaware that the tin contained only sand. On another occasion, an uncle might drop an envelope on the ground with a casual comment – 'there's a letter from your girl friend'. The writing on the envelope confirmed that it was from his sweetheart, but again the exercise of discipline – the long wait until the men departed, the excitement of grabbing up the envelope, only to discover that the men had removed the letter to offer it to him the next day, perhaps.

Becoming a Bush boy is an important step in the life of the Ngaanyatjarra. It is the beginning of manhood and a time to set aside childish things and assume new responsibilities. One of their duties was to pass on songs and fundamental dance routines to the younger boys, and it was to such an occasion that I was invited.

At dusk, Joseph and Richard came to the house to lead me through the scrub to a secluded site four kilometres from camp; far from the ears of the women and girls.

A ring of boys had gathered around a low fire and I recognised half the boys of my class. I tossed a couple of packets of cigarettes and biscuits to Dennis who shared them around the group. In return I was given a mulga stick to beat the hard earth in rhythmic accompaniment to the singing. The firelight flared, casting a warm glow on the dancers and the swaying bodies of the singing boys, who would be chanting their

Senior boys digging out a water-hole.

multiplication tables with much less enthusiasm the following morning.

That night was a further introduction to thousands of years of Aboriginal tradition; tradition that was now seriously threatened by western influences. Wise guidance by the old men would make the youth valued members of their Ngaanyatjarra groups. Wise teaching in the school would support the authority of tribal law, while implanting the skills to survive in modern Australia. With good teachers in the bush and in the classroom they would learn that both schools were important.

One gave them proof of their own existence and made them aware of the authority they could exercise within their own communities. The other sought to give them access to a knowledge of a different law and different type of authority. For without this dual knowledge, the individual would be forced to deny one and retreat into the other. Even in 1966 it was obvious that the survival of the Ngaanyatjarra would be decided by the ability to command both sets of knowledge.

I had finished breakfast the following morning when a missionary came over to the school house.

'Two of those big boys wouldn't shower this morning so I said, no shower, no breakfast! They can stay hungry if they are too lazy to wash!'

It was difficult for the missionary to understand that it was bad luck to wash off the body designs that had been carefully painted on the night before. Like the Ash Wednesday cross on the forehead of the Catholics it was better that it wear off than be washed away. So the boys sat outside the mission for a few days until the incident was forgotten.

The Bush boys had been out of the camp for several months when the formal ceremonies began and every day for a week the men retired to the sacred grounds beyond the sight and hearing of the women. At last the decision on the initiates was made and that afternoon Billy stopped off at the fence to pass on the news and invite me to the evening ceremony. Mary and the girls were not included in the invitation.

A crowd of almost three hundred men, women and children had gathered at the ceremonial grounds about three kilometres from the mission. There was an atmosphere of expectancy and undertones of hushed and excited talk. The early part of this ceremony was not secret and the men had permitted the young boys, women and girls to be present. The children were surprised to see me and my presence seemed to embarrass some. Others chortled 'Good-day, Sir!', and laughed to see a Wyalpula in their midst.

Throughout the preceding days, the initiates had lain under a blanket in the scorching sun, listening to the songs of the elders and sensing the vibrant dances forbidden to their view. There should have been three to go through the law this night, but when the men came for the boys, James had gone off with the younger boys to hunt and ride the wild horses that had been trapped at a nearby waterhole. The rules were strict. If a novice was not prepared to attend the preliminaries, then he could not be accepted for the finals. The old men were adamant. The youth had acted as a boy — he was obviously not ready to become a man. On the night of the initiation ceremony, James' father argued for his son's inclusion, and when his entreaties failed, he exploded into frustrated fury and indiscriminately hurled a barrage of spears, which caused a few anxious moments as the crowd ducked for cover. He stamped off into the darkness as everyone came together for the opening ceremonies.

At a signal from the senior men, the bonfires flared and, to the astonished gasps of the women and the loud cries from the immediate family, the initiates appeared to emerge from the flames and ran into the darkness beyond the rim of firelight. Symbolically, the boys had died when they were grabbed by the men and declared Bush boys. Their appearance at the ceremonies drew loud and prolonged wailing from all the adult Ngaanyatjarra gathered there. For almost ten minutes the wails continued, then from the fringes of the firelight a compact group of painted men appeared, their lusty singing rising above the wails. The women's grief gave way to consternation as senior men moved amongst the crowd and ordered the women and children to leave and in less than twenty minutes only the initiated men, the initiates and I remained. Long into the night I joined with the others striking the ground in the rhythmic fashion I had learned at the Bush boys camps.*

I came to realise that the nights spent with the Bush boys had been a means of the Ngaanyatjarra assessing my suitability to attend an important ceremony. Wyalpula who behaved like children with foolish laughter and inquisitive cameras were frequently categorised with the women and children and effectively excluded from any advanced ceremonies. My acceptance by the men enhanced my status in the community and certainly made the senior children more responsive to my presence in the classroom.

---

*   *To describe the ceremony beyond the departure of the women and children would be a violation of trust and furthermore, this material would be offensive to the Ngaanyatjarra and other desert groups.*

MELINDA'S DIARY

19 October
Yesterday after tea when I was going towards Phyliss camp. I saw Harold coming along the road towards his camp, and also he had something inside his shirt. But I was too busy helping Phyliss to make a wiltja properley. But when I came to see him, he pulled one fat mother rabbit out of his shirt, and also he had little bird inside his pocket and he gave me the little bird to cooked it at the red ashes only for myself.

26 October
Yesterday after tea when I was going toward my camp. But I saw a lovely clean sand beside a pirickle and also it was a mouse hole so I went down to get the crowbar, and after that I came back with the little crow-bar, and I was digging I saw some little pink mice sleeping on the warm grass under the soft ground beside some bushy trees. So I did took the little pink mice down to my Auntie's camp beside the trees.

CHAPTER SEVENTEEN
The End of the School Year

During the last weeks of term the heat intensified under the aluminium school roof, sending the temperature soaring above forty degrees. The school term had been long and tiring; the children were listless. Everyone, including the teachers, was flagging and the heat only served to add to their lethargy. The final months of the year were the most difficult for the children — long hours in the classroom, merging into long weeks before the Christmas vacation. By the second week of November they began to doggedly slow down their school output, for already their thoughts had pushed ahead to the exhilarating freedom of seven weeks in the bush, hunting and gathering, free of the impositions of the church and the school. For the girls, it was a time when they would resume their tribal education in desert survival — a time when they would build bush wiltjas, chase lizards, dig for honey ants and accompany the women on their daily quest for food. The boys would use the time to reinforce their deep empathy with the land, as preparation for the time when they must accept the responsibilities of 'the law'.

It was late November, the class was busy at maths when the keen ears of the children picked up urgent cries from the compound. The concerned glances that flashed across the classroom and the rapid exchange of dialect alerted me to an approaching crisis.

'What is it, Stanley?'

The boy's face was inscrutable as he carefully phrased his reply. 'People call out big storm coming'.

I glanced out of the window and along the Laverton track. The sky was clear. The older children sensed my puzzlement.

'Storm come from hills, sir'!

Walking out into the passage I saw, through the window, the crest of dust storm billowing above the stunted mulgas, awesome, rolling forward, swallowing trees and hills in its monstrous path.

The irregular profile of the Warburton Ranges was obscured by a brick red tidal wave that had already encircled Brown Range. For a moment I stood and watched, entranced. Then suddenly the visible world ended with a pall of dust and a swirling roar. David and the senior boys had already run the length of the school passage slamming the windows shut to keep the dust from the desks and books. The children sat, awed by the wind that thrust spears of dust into the sunset gloom of the room. These were children accustomed to sitting out the struggles of nature, but as the storm grew in intensity so too did their fear that the flimsy aluminium walls would be crushed and hurled down on top of them. The dust hung so heavily in the room that eventually I could see only the two front rows of children. Then, just as suddenly as it came, the storm passed and the class erupted onto the playground, releasing pent up fears in jubilant yells and high pitched laughter.

As the year drew to a close I began to take a stock of what I had learned at Warburton Ranges and the impact the community had made on my life and my family. By mid year the early traumas and uncertainties had given way to a new confidence and I discovered facets of teaching that were previously unknown to me. It seemed as though I had merely been acting out a role, a Teachers' College model, scripted on antiquated philosophies and rehearsed before audiences that responded on cue. At Warburton I learnt that a teacher's function was to share knowledge with the class not merely to dispense it, and I discovered that if I became interested in the children's experiences they were more inclined to listen to me. By bringing the environment into the classroom I had lessened the bias of the Europeanised curriculum and textbooks. On many occasions we took the lessons out of doors. By writing words in the dust, counting trees and reading the labels of tinned food, the effect of school went beyond the classroom, as children began applying the new learned skills to their everyday lives. Education became less of a Wyalpula activity, and as the children began to see relevance in the lessons their enthusiasm for learning increased.

Frequently we teachers try to impose our values of honesty and integrity on children without considering that they may have a different concept of honesty and integrity.

Many times since Warburton, I have sat in an Aboriginal classroom and watched the teacher write answers on the board and from my position I have noted eight or nine of the class quietly fill in the blank spaces or change their answers. This was not learning, and this was not an application of traditional Aboriginal social sharing. If we make the classroom a place where only right answers are tolerated, we encourage children to give us only right answers and not understanding. It was a new experience to find myself permitting children to assume the roles of instructor in the classroom, using the home dialect to convey to others what was not understood. This was tried initially in art, where little children would watch the older ones sketching, and later the seniors would walk around the classroom and quietly indicate to the novices why a tree didn't look quite right, or why a bird was lopsided. Later I permitted the children to apply this to other subject areas, particularly mathematics. Number, and mathematics in general, was the greatest challenge in the desert school and, although years later I can say that I have a better understanding of the problem, I have few new answers.

There were times when the children didn't want to participate in the

Children at Warburton, 1978.

activity that I had decided upon. On such occasions the common response
was 'Which one, Sir?' For example I may decide that today we'd work on
page twenty-five of a text book. I would say — 'Let's open up our books at
page twenty-five'. 'Twenty-five' A child would call out, 'Which one?'
'Which one, Sir? which one? this one?' Pages would fly in a flurry of
useless activity. Many of the children, although they could count to
twenty-five, did not have a concept of twenty-five when it was applied to
practical situations. Number had been learned by rote; it had little
meaning. The children would open up at page one and follow through one,
two, three, four, up to twenty-five, but if they wanted to be difficult they
would open it at random or just flick through the pages hoping twenty-five
would appear. It would be a testing of my patience to remain calm, write
the number twenty-five on the board and tell them to look for that
number. Although I solved the immediate problem, it didn't dispel my
concern that I had a group of children whose number concept was
different from mine and therefore, it was exasperating to try and teach
them maths.
    Mathematics seemed to be an area where the children only achieved
success after years of solid drilling of tables and number combinations.
Teachers before and since have told me that Aborigines are poor at
mathematics because their language is limited in counting to four. This was
not quite true. The Ngaanyatjarra used a word — kutju which denoted one
person — me; kutjarra meant a pair — two persons; kutjarra kutjarra meant
two and two more, and beyond that tjurta which meant 'many'. The

limited language terms for number is not sufficient reason to excuse our failure to teach mathematics effectively to Aboriginal children. Perhaps we should look more closely at the traditional Aboriginal concepts of time, space, mass and measurement and develop teaching strategies that build on the existing concepts, rather than our present policy of developing new concepts in children to prepare them for the old strategies. We should also look closely at the way Aboriginal children are educated outside the classroom. There are major differences between Wyalpula and Ngaanyatjarra child rearing practices. The desert child learns skills for specific experiences while the white child learns rules that may be applied to a range of experiences that may occur in the future. The white child learns at an early age to use questioning techniques, to challenge and to expand his creative thinking. The Ngaanyatjarra child is not encouraged to question adults. His family, unlike his teachers, will not ask him seemingly aimless questions — 'Today is Tuesday, children. What is today?' Neither will he be exposed to hypothetical situations that are supposed to stimulate his imagination — 'What would you have done if it rained yesterday?' It is impossible for the Ngaanyatjarra child to conceptualise such a non-existent experience.

The success or failure of the desert school teacher is often decided within the first four weeks after his arrival. By talking to all manner of people before I left Perth for Warburton I realised that I had to have either a dynamic personality or a few gimmicks up the sleeve. Lacking in the first I relied on the second. The goldfish, magnifying glasses, magnets, science tricks and pop records attracted tremendous attention amongst the school children. So too did my model aircraft, although the similarity between the roar of the motor and the chatter of a twirling sacred board caused initial concern amongst the men. Gimmicks and dynamic personalities may be good opening gambits but beyond that there must be more enduring teaching qualities.

I began to realise that the effective teacher of Aboriginal children must have a gregarious nature, without being bombastic. He is tolerant of cultural differences without being paternalistic; demanding of children but not domineering; he is warm and supportive of the child's hesitant efforts; sensitive to the changing moods of the child that signal impending problems, yet fair in his response. He is conscious of the influence of community conflict on the classroom behaviour but is not overwhelmed by the social issues that lie beyond his authority. He avoids resorting to emotional and physical brutality in the classroom, yet is not to be cowed by anger directed at himself; he is respectful of the wishes of the elders, and acknowledges the authority of the important female and the male law holders, but he must also exhibit qualities that will attract the respect of the adults and children of the community.

The teacher must be prepared to become involved in the currents of community life and in turn, by warmth, friendliness and patient encouragement bring the community to an active involvement in the school, not merely as visitors but as partners in the policy making and participants in the teaching process. The effective teacher becomes conversant with the child's home language so that he, as a learner, may become aware of the difficulties of learning a second language. He also comes to realise that the child's first language acts as a filter on the second language, to influence the way he speaks it and how he applies its rules of grammar, thus accenting his speech and inhibiting his written expression.

The teacher of Aboriginal children must come to understand how people grow within a cultural framework and develop values and attitudes that are influenced by their distinctive socialisation. The teacher who is prepared to observe with care will begin to realise that the Aboriginal child may have different pre-school experiences to the Anglo-Australian child. He may not have played the games that teach white children the basic rules of interaction within the classroom: of taking turns; waiting to be called; responding to questions and instructions. Consequently the teacher must discover what the child regards as acceptable and unacceptable behaviours. To sit beside a child conveys warmth whereas to sit opposite is to present a physical confrontation, with an emphasis on eye contact so often seen as threatening. Young Aboriginal children will not sit and listen as readily as European children, for instructions such as 'listen to me!' are uncommon in the home where a child may choose not to listen to an adult. Because the children are less likely to respond to verbal instructions the effective teacher will use strategies that utilise the child's highly developed visual skills. The teacher must understand that the Aboriginal child may see things differently to the European child and should not be expected to respond in terms outside his or her cultural experience. The perceptive teacher can work within the framework of the child's cultural language and experience. There should be fewer demands for the school beginner to conform to western standards of behaviour. Desk work should be minimised and the time allocated to group mat activities should be increased. The children should be given frequent opportunities to talk about their families, animals, birds and bush foods so that every day they feel good just being at school. The discerning teacher will quickly come to appreciate the importance of family to the young child and will patiently answer personal questions about his own family.

The effective teacher seeks to understand the culture of the child, the religious base of the community's beliefs, the richness of the music, oral literature and history of the people and the region; and in so doing he discovers the underlying values of the child's society and how these values may unconsciously be set in opposition to the values expressed by the classroom teacher. Yet, in exploring the depths of tribal knowledge, there is an inherent danger in the Anglo-Australian teacher becoming enamoured by the apparent simplicity of the Aboriginal lifestyle and, in so doing, slip his own cultural anchors and become adrift and disoriented.

The successful teacher of Aboriginal children has an engaging humour, which he combines with the sense to laugh with people and never at them. He has the ability to be flexible in his classroom organisation so that he can respond rapidly to change; he is adaptive to the needs of individual children and possesses a creative resourcefulness that will enable him to convert every situation into an enriching experience. The ideal teacher in a cross-cultural classroom is practical; he sets objectives that are demanding yet realistic, challenging yet satisfying. Finally he accepts the limitations imposed by the present, yet anticipates the needs of the child as an adult decision maker of the future.

These were ideals, but by the end of the year I knew I was a long way from achieving many of them.

December came quickly. The exams required by the authorities had been set, marked and the result sheets placed in the desk drawers ready for the incoming teachers. The partly used workbooks were neatly piled in cupboards to be handed out to the children the following year and every desk was polished and shining. With very little ceremony the children were dismissed for the year, then the classrooms and school were locked and the keys left with the missionaries. Soon we would head south again to spend the seven week Christmas vacation with relatives and enjoy the cool waters of the coastal beaches.

The morning after school broke up, the family groups which constituted most of the Ngaanyatjarra population, gathered at the open ground outside our house. Bundles of bedding were piled in heaps, each loosely tied with bits of string, wire and rope. Billy cans for water and tea, dented and blackened, topped the loads. The women sat together talking for a while, then they loaded the bundles upon their shoulders, slung the babies in the calici across their hips and, with the children trailing behind, doggedly followed their menfolk into the bush. The destination would be one of a number of watering places within a hundred kilometre radius of the mission. Upon reaching the bush camps, the families built wiltjas that had the delightful fragrance of freshly cut mulga branches, and relived the traditional lifestyle. At times the urge to be alone with the Dreaming and the home country took a family far from the mission wells and windmills and into the regions where their survival depended upon an unerring knowledge of natural resources and an ability to instinctively gauge the effects of drought on waterholes and harvest foods.

Far from the mission school the children continued their education but now it was education where the lessons were those of survival, and careless students were punished not by a cross in their workbooks, but by the rigours of hunger and thirst and even death, in an environment that was intolerant of human error.

The six seater charter plane arrived two days after school closed and by then the Aboriginal families had moved out to the vacation outcamps. As we walked towards the landing field the mission was deserted, with a silence broken only by the rumble of drums as the pilot refuelled the plane. The compound was emptied of people, the shade beneath the verandah store was abandoned. No dogs snarled, no cries of men ruptured the morning stillness. Only the missionaries and the Native Welfare officer's family bade us farewell as the plane, enveloped in dust, rose above the Warburton Ranges and headed for Perth.

I had expected to return to Warburton Ranges the following year but as the school needed a fourth teacher, I paid the penalty for having a non-teaching wife. The Education Department decided to transfer me and send in two married couples, all teachers. I found out only after I left Warburton and despite my pleas, the Director General would neither reconsider the transfer nor pay my way back to Warburton to pack. The week after Christmas I hitch-hiked the two thousand kilometres to Warburton to pack our belongings. Getting out of Warburton posed more serious problems and after I had been stranded for nearly three weeks, Mary phoned the local Member of Parliament. This caused the Education Department to relent and charter a plane to bring me home. After Warburton, we went to another Aboriginal mission school located along a tidal river in the north-west of Australia, and the baggage I packed at Warburton in January arrived by lugger seven months later.

MELINDA'S DIARY

CHAPTER EIGHTEEN
Warburton Revisited

I have returned to Warburton Ranges on four occasions since 1966 and it has been possible to observe the effects of rapid change on the lifestyle of the population. The four major agents of change appear to have been motor vehicles, social welfare payments, the outcamp movement and, to a lesser degree, education.

Ranking next in importance to tribal law is the Ngaanyatjarra's obsession with anything on wheels. Vehicles are used for hunting kangaroo and bush turkeys, carting firewood, visiting other settlements for ceremonies and simply for the pleasure of joyriding. On a five hundred kilometres stretch of road east of Laverton, I counted more than one hundred abandoned vehicles and at Warburton there is a massive scrapyard of cars and trucks.

The extension of Australian welfare benefits to Aborigines has provided the desert communities with a regular economy that ensures that the population is better fed than under the semi-subsistence diet of the mission days. Adults are better clothed and the begging of cigarette butts, clothing and food from the whites has virtually ceased. However, the inflow of government money for housing has affected only a minority, for most of the families still live in the bush and iron wiltjas of the mission days.

In 1972 the United Aboriginal Mission relinquished its control of the settlement and contingents of white government workers moved in — each responsible to a different department — with little co-operation between their respective groups. At the same time the Federal Government undertook to sink water bores at places which in the pre-mission days had been significant tribal campsites. By 1975 the outcamps movement was well under way and the Aboriginal population began to return to their home countries. As a consequence the population of Warburton was reduced to one quarter of its 1966 number.

During 1966, the Mission had begun to pass back to the parents the responsibility for caring for their children and this was fully achieved in 1970. Without free food as a motivating force, there was a detectable change in the attitudes of children and the community towards the school and its teachers. These early changes can be traced through the school records.

Warburton Ranges, 1979.

August 1969. A parent's meeting was held on the school lawns. Thirty parents attended to voice their objections to the filming of the mission and children by a visitor. The parents complained that sacred sites, taboo areas and the photographed images of deceased persons were treated as curiosities. They were fed up with specialists and survey teams.

September 1969. Before the start of school all the children were withdrawn from the playground by parents because of a dining room dispute.

September 1969. Softball and volley ball were being played at school and a cricket pitch was laid on the school oval.

March 1970. Enrolment 100. The parents, school staff and mission were co-operating in drawing up the policy and rules for the school.

April 1970. The children's clothing was poor in quality. The senior boys were wearing long pants over their shorts as status symbols. Any boys without long trousers stayed away from school.

July 1970. The children were showered for the first time in a month and given new clothes in anticipation of a government visit.

July 1970. Instances of petrol sniffing reported.

During the eight years that followed there was a general deterioration in the standard of education. The older children resisted being sent away for education and established a reputation for being aggressive and unco-operative. Their presence around the settlements encouraged the senior primary school boys to absent themselves from school. The increasing mobility between the outcamps and Warburton greatly reduced the children's exposure to education and often their attendances were interspersed with months of absences, making it impossible for the teachers to develop continuous learning programs. Petrol sniffing became a serious problem and remains so. Most of the children under twelve years sniffed and several were serious addicts.

It was commonplace to see children with meat tins containing a small amount of petrol. Others carried petrol soaked rags in their pockets which they frequently sniffed. One boy was asphyxiated when he crept into a small cupboard to sniff undisturbed and closed the door, but his death did not deter the sniffers. When children are high on petrol, they become aggressive towards the teachers. On settlements in the Northern Territory, where sniffing extends to the older groups, bashings and pack rapes have been reported.

One of my visits to Warburton coincided with a sitting of the Royal Commission of Inquiry into allegations of police ill-treatment of desert tribesmen at Skull Creek in Laverton on January the fifth 1975, when forty men, fifteen women and twenty-one children travelling to attend religious ceremonies at Wiluna were confronted by twenty-six police officers. All the men, with the exception of a few elders, were arrested and charged with offences. The report published as *The Report of the Laverton Royal Commission* (1975) concluded that the police had acted wrongfully and the charges were false.

I attended a session at which Richard, a former pupil, gave evidence. The small demountable classroom was barely adequate to accommodate the double row of commissioners, recorders, legal officers, welfare agents and the anthropological advisers. The witnesses were ushered in and hesitantly gave their evidence. It was a painstakingly slow process. Only one witness was fully heard on the first day. The Commission encountered difficulties resulting from a language barrier that required translators to be present; tribal restrictions that caused men to hesitate to give evidence in front of women recorders; the refusal of young men to identify elders by name; and a confusion caused by the fear among older men that the hearing was some sort of a court which may send them away to jail. I listened to Richard give his evidence. A problem of identification arose when he replied that a man he saw wore a grey uniform.

'Could he identify a similar colour in the room?'

'No.'

'Where was there a similar colour?'

'Worn by the policeman outside the door!'

The constable was asked to enter the room.

'Khaki!' The interrogator loudly identified the colour and a ripple of laughter erupted from many of the whites present.

Richard didn't laugh and neither did the other Ngaanyatjarra men in the public chairs along the wall. The Chairman of the Commission hastened to reassure the witness that such laughter was not to be taken as an insult.

Outside the temporary inquiry room I watched the young men and women passing. They were better dressed than they had been before. Leather gear and denim was popular and some girls were wearing slacks, inconceivable a decade before. Amongst the men there were also notable changes. No one asked for my cigarette butts nor even for a cigarette. In fact some of the men that I offered a smoke, politely refused because they were non-smokers. In the society of 1966 they were expected to accept these gifts if not for themselves, then on behalf of older relatives. I was amazed to see younger women with their own packets of cigarettes offering them around a peer group without having the packet commandeered by the males.

The major changes were in the generation I taught, now grown up. All the pupils of my class of '66 had travelled beyond the Western Desert, to the nickel town of Laverton to the south, and to Alice Springs to the east. Some had travelled to the far north, seeking work or attending ceremonies, but the yearning for the home country brought all but a few back to the tribal communities in the desert. Several of the men had been delegates to Land Rights conventions in the Australian capital at Canberra or in State Capitals. Others had attended training courses in towns and cities.

All but three of my boys of 1966 had accumulated lists of charges and convictions for violence and drunkenness. Four had served prison sentences for murder or manslaughter. Prison did not have the same social stigma for the Ngaanyatjarra as it did for the Wyalpula. Prison was even becoming a status symbol for the youth, substituting to some extent the rites of passage to manhood that initiation had provided in earlier years. Prison was the finishing school where the English language skills, implanted in the classroom, were extended and refined. With Aboriginal children there is often a high correlation between English skills and the time spent in hospital. Similarly with the adults, the best English speakers had usually served prison sentences, and occasionally these became the spokespersons for their communities. This was not so much an expression of their status in the law, as the elders' confidence in their ability to parry the questions of the Wyalpula and present the communities' demands forcefully.

Of the girls of 1966, nearly all were married and living on one of the small settlements across the desert. Occasionally, as I passed a group of women, one would hail me shyly with, 'Do you know who I am, Mr Green?', and I would search the face for clues and usually admit defeat before being enlightened and introduced to the new generation of desert children. Ada was a very successful teacher aide in one of the settlement schools, Melinda managed a community store and Joan had gathered about herself a delightful family of five children. Andrea's story was a sad one. After she left school she became a teacher aide and during one vacation stayed with us at Perth. Two years later tragedy struck. Her uncle and then

Mrs Laidlaw and her children.

her father died and she became part of the alcoholic flotsam of the mining
towns, living each day only for the joys of the shared bottle.

There was far more food available for purchase at the Warburton
store and more money. A weekly 'money bag' flight brought in the social
welfare cheques, which included family allowances, unemployment, age
and invalid pensions. Bin scavenging had ceased and only the dogs fought
over the dregs in the tins discarded by the dining room, which fed the
children free, without the obligation of school attendance or of payment
by parents. Fewer spears were used in hunting and the several old men
attending the Royal Commission Inquiry carried their spears as status
symbols of a passing generation. Yet there was a brisk trade in woomeras,
spears and artefacts which were bought by the store and consigned to the
cities. Rifles were also kept out of sight and only carried through the
settlement when the men went off to hunt for kangaroo, whose meat was
preferred to the thin and often tough slices of frozen grilling steak bought
at the store.

The function of most of the Mission buildings of 1966 had changed.
The church, and the dormitory buildings had been demolished. The stone
and mud mission buildings were housing families, as was the garage where
the men had once furtively played cards for bullets. The hospital was now
a home for Stanley's family; he had bought his own 16 mm sound
projector and controlled the movies at two dollars per head admission. The
screen erected by the mining company was still in use and the patrons sat
on green lawn in the lea of the school building.

Mrs Laidlaw's house, 1975.

The Native Welfare officer's home was occupied by a member of the Community Council, who was also the community warden, empowered by the Council to maintain order amongst the group. In 1966 he had been one of the outspoken young men of the settlement, asking for housing for his family and his people and deploring the system which promised educational equality in town high schools yet forced them back to a squalid existence at Warburton.

At first, the sight of the former mission and government houses being occupied by Ngaanyatjarra families brought a feeling of satisfaction. But a quick count showed only nine houses had been built since 1966. The imbalance of housing did not seem so apparent in 1966. There was then a sort of acceptance by both Wyalpula and Ngaanyatjarra of our respective places. We expected to live in houses and never really considered the needs of the increasing number of educated young men and women. The disparity in accommodation now loomed as one of the major social issues at Warburton. The four teacher aides working in the school were given equal teaching status by the principal, who refused to regard them merely as aides. One was my pupil in 1966. Another was the Community Council chairman, a third was a talented and extremely confident Warburton woman who was separated from her white husband. All were making a vital contribution to the future of the Warburton community, yet their accommodation was appalling by accepted Australian standards.

After the Government employees had breakfasted, the work parties began to assemble under white supervisors. A latrine block was under construction, badly located on a high rise of land, at what must eventually be on the opposite side of the settlement to the Aboriginal housing. Fifty yards away some men sat outside the project officer's house, awaiting news of an aircraft's arrival, while the community secretary took the morning radio schedule with Kalgoorlie, sending and receiving telegrams, despatching urgent orders for supplies and receiving advice that the Flying Doctor would call later that day for a sick child. In the fuel compound, where petrol cost twice the city price, a dozen men worked under the supervision of the project officer to erect the framework of the vehicle workshop. Two men with crowbars chipped away at the hard calcite rock to sink a service well in the floor of the shed. At some future date, another building was planned to provide a store for spare parts collected from the trucks and cars that littered the settlement. Many of the vehicle defects had been minor; a flat battery, a punctured tube or a cracked distributor, but in the absence of spare parts the cars were abandoned then cannibalised for parts for other cars. The windows were smashed by children and the bodies left to rust. A few old station wagons had been converted into family dwellings. There seemed little concern at the monetary loss incurred and a few weeks later several men would pool their social welfare cheques to fly one of their group to Kalgoorlie to buy another car for cash and begin the terminal journey to Warburton.

The store had opened and a crowd gathered to purchase supplies. The Ngaanyatjarra no longer used the prop-drop window of 1966, but shopped at the side entrance once reserved exclusively for the use of Wyalpula. The range of goods was considerable; canned motor oil, frozen meat, eggs, sliced bread, toys and fresh fruit. A large bi-lingual notice stated boldly that no credit would be given, but many of the working men were in debt to the greater part of their wages. The store was run by a white member of the settlement. After the missionaries left, the community tried to manage the store but without white supervision it suffered a serious loss. This was not a matter of mismanagement but a yielding to tribal pressures and the demands by the shop assistants' relatives for free supplies.

I drove to the far side of the airstrip and searched for Billy's camp amongst the dozens of rusting iron shelters within which the women made damper with store bought flour; many using dented hub caps as mixing bowls. I found Billy directing his family in the manufacture of artefacts; the youngest wife chipping at a wooden bowl while the children smoothed miniature woomeras with chips of glass. I stood off and called his name. He looked up and scowled at the Wyalpula intrusion. Then as he linked my face with the past he beckoned me to his camp and greeted me with a warm embrace. We talked briefly of old times, of the artefact trade, of his two sons just released from gaol, whom he spoke of with affection, trust and caring. He accepted with pleasure my gift of a plug of chewing tobacco, unobtainable at the settlement, and sadly shook his head over the two spears snuggled in the grass, made from jarrah timber brought in for building. They had no sale prospect at the Mission store which sought only true bush spears. He made no mention of the son killed in a car roll-over or another son who died after drinking duplicating spirit stolen from the school.

One of my visits to the Western Desert followed a Yulpurri ceremony at Warburton. This was a gathering of all tribal groups from the many desert settlements for sacred/secret ceremonies and more than eight hundred people had set up camps around Warburton. With so much happening the children refused to attend school and for two consecutive days the teachers and aides sat in the empty rooms preparing charts and marking work books.

On the third day the Community Council called a meeting at the school to discuss the truancy problems. A school sub-committee was formed and the children were brought to the school to receive a talk by the councillors. It was agreed that several of the men would drive around the settlement and camps each morning to bring in the children. The following week-end, a town Aboriginal made an illegal liquor run, selling wine on the Warburton settlement for forty dollars per gallon flagon. Fights resulting from the binge affected school attendance for the next two days. Over a three week period the children attended nine days out of fifteen; full attendance on any of the nine days was never achieved.

I attended a second Council meeting held in the open. The men and school teachers discussed the problem of continuing truancy. The teachers said they could not teach if the children were not at school. One of the parents said 'Maybe the teachers should go out and pick up the children'. Another man opposed this. 'Teacher's job is to teach at school not to chase kids. It's the mothers, it's the fathers who have to send their kids to school, have to make them go.'

Someone else proposed that the men go down and pick up the children each morning. It was pointed out that this was already being done, but the children heard the vehicle approaching and scattered to the bush or hid amongst the buildings. It was then proposed that the Education Department be approached to buy a bus for the school. Others agreed this was a good idea as it was too cold for children to come to school. Another man complained that his children wouldn't go to school because the teachers wouldn't let them out to the toilet. The teachers responded that when they let children out to go to the toilet, they rarely came back, but if the parents could give assurances that their children would return to school then the problem could be overcome. The teachers also attributed truancy to a disco that was being operated at the dining room, for the children preferred disco music and dancing to attending school. The men decided that the disco would be kept closed while school was on. The community was beginning to realise that it was their settlement and that if Wyalpula were conducting an activity they disagreed with, they had the power to stop them.

Getting children to school and keeping them there was a game played between the teachers and children. Each morning several of the men, and sometimes the teachers drove around the settlement gathering up

Warakuna outcamp, 1978.

the school children. School starting time was officially nine o'clock, but an hour later teachers were still bringing in small groups of children. The school day began when there were enough children in the building to make teaching worthwhile. Lessons continued without a break until lunchtime and the normal morning recess period was not observed because as soon as the children were dismissed into the playground they continued on to the camp. The teachers were deeply concerned at the absenteeism as well as the children's behaviour and tried to compensate by a heavy emphasis on basic literacy and numeracy skills. In so doing they were inclined to sacrifice the close interaction between teacher and child, both in the classroom and the playground. And without close exchanges there is no communication and disinterest and failure are the inevitable consequences.

It was a school where I heard no children singing. No basketballs were tossed in the yard or footballs kicked and it seemed that the situation had moved beyond the point of compromise.

A prisoner and warder type of conflict existed in the school. No violence — just a game that each played. For the teachers it was terribly serious — getting children to school, keeping them there and teaching them. The classroom doors were bolted when the last child was in the room and on the occasions when the teacher left the room, the door was bolted from the outside to prevent children escaping, and I even found myself locked in with the class.

Escape became a challenge for the children and they seemed to delight in devising ways in which they could get out of the classroom.

Sometimes a toilet request was used as a ruse to escape to camp, or a distraction in one part of the class that took the teacher away from the door and allowed a child to make a break for freedom. Sometimes the teacher would go after these children, shouting at them, and they would sullenly return to the classroom.

Six of the older girls had entered the classroom carrying their story wires bent around their necks. As they read their books, or walked around the classroom reading any chart that took their eye, they tapped each word with their story wire until the charts and books were peppered with holes from the repeated tapping. On the mat the boys separated themselves into a compact group. Some leaned against the back wall nonchalantly watching the teacher, a challenging look and then a quick attempt to break through the door, the teacher responded, the children withdrew and laughed. It was a game, for they realised that any sudden movement towards the door caused a frenzy of activity from the teacher. In the middle of a lesson there was a clatter of desks deliberately banged. A child was angry and showing her anger towards the teacher by banging her desk. Almost at once other children joined in. Desks were lifted and banged in unison, the teacher shouted for silence, shouted for control, the children laughed and stopped. On other occasions children used a pact of silence and refused to answer any questions put to them. It was the children who controlled their own noise, it was the children who decided when they would make a noise and when they would stop.

The senior classroom was in the same room, in the same building as in 1966, but fibreboard covered the aluminium walls. The western windows through which Stanley and Richard had looked down the track for the truck so many years before were now boarded up. There were electric fans and fluorescent lights, but the desks were unchanged and the floor was still the cold concrete. No heaters had been installed and the rooms were as uninviting as before.

The teacher presented a simple maths problem and the children chorused their response. The teacher singled out specific children to answer but this was not always successful and they seemed to give the first number that came into their head. A question, 'What is $4 + 1$?' brought a volley of answers — 'one' 'four!' 'three!' 'seven!' 'twelve!' None gave the right answer. This response occurs because answering adult questions is not part of the Ngaanyatjarra child's socialization. Obviously the teacher wanted an answer, so in their eagerness to please the children gave him a barrage of answers. Experience had proven that the teacher knows the correct answer and will select the response that agreed with his. In this situation a correct answer occurred by chance rather than design. It was part of a game to please the teacher, for in Aboriginal society people do not ask questions when they know the answers.

The classroom was a babble of noise, a mixture of dialect and English, interspersed with shouts as the children called across the room to each other, sometimes to attract attention of a friend or the teacher, occasionally to ask a question relevant to the lesson.

There was a noticeable change in behaviour as the lessons alternated

between the desks and the mat. At the desks the children were more
unruly and aggressive towards each other. The soft swear word drew an
immediate response as a pencil was sharply jabbed in the ribs of the child.
There was a sudden sob, and a chair overturned as the attacker rushed to
escape the classroom. The class greeted the situation with a mixture of
responses; some with a silent questioning in their eyes, others with ripples
of laughter.

As they finished their lessons the children moved onto a mat area at
the rear of the room where they sat reading magazines and library books.
Here no desks were banged and no rulers were rattled in simulated sword
fights. There was just a low interchange between groups and pairs and it
made me wonder if desks and chairs were really necessary.

By 1976, the Ngaanyatjarra population of Warburton had
fragmented to form five desert settlements located at Warburton Ranges,
Blackstone Ranges, Warakuna, near the Rawlinson Ranges, and Wingellina
in the Tonkinson Ranges, near the South Australian border. Each
settlement had a building that was referred to as 'school' but only the first
three had qualified teachers.

The Education Department responded to the outcamp movement by
appointing itinerate teachers who were each expected to maintain two
schools concurrently — up to two hundred kilometres apart. The number
of children at the outcamp schools ranged between six and fifty six and
the daily period of attendance was anything from twenty minutes to three
hours, depending upon the weather, camp activities and the opening time
of the store, which usually terminated the lessons for the day. At
Blackstone and Warakuna, the teachers lived in small caravans equipped
with showers but no toilets, so in common with the community they
squatted on the ground beyond the perimeter of the camp.

Petrol generators were provided but these were rarely used because
the noise irritated the Ngaanyatjarra and the fuel was too accessible to the
young petrol sniffers. At both settlements school was conducted in poorly
equipped buildings erected by the community. One teacher direct from
training college taught in a spinifex grass shed that later burnt down. His
only teaching equipment was a blackboard and easel, a wooden storage
box and a fluid duplicator that he did not know how to assemble. He did
assemble it months later but its use was banned because three young men
died from drinking duplicating fluid as an alcohol substitute. The outcamp
school was so different to any experiences he had as a student that he was
unsure what he should be teaching or whether he really was teaching at all.

I was invited to Blackstone community to meet my ex-pupils and I
spent the morning in the school. It was bitterly cold, with a southerly
wind sweeping across the desert. By eight o'clock five children had
gathered at the teacher's caravan and huddled out of the wind. The teacher
walked across to the school, the children followed and soon there were
twelve who sat around a small fire for a while before moving inside. The
younger children and the pre-schoolers clustered around the Aboriginal
teacher aide, the older children sat with the teacher. All the work was

Teacher's caravan home, Blackstone Ranges. 1979.

carried out sitting on the concrete floor and occasionally a child would get up on the pretext of going to the toilet and linger around the fire until called back inside.

The outcamp schools at Jamieson, Blackstone, Wingellina and Warakuna had been built by the parents who regarded them as community property. In 1979 the first air-conditioned transportable classrooms arrived but lacked furniture, equipment, books or pencils. The teachers of the neighbouring schools across the borders in South Australia and the Northern Territory offered supplies. However, officials in Perth instructed the Western Australian teachers to refuse such offers and have no further communication with inter-state schools. This was an incredible order, for the families, being unencumbered by politics and protocol, regularly moved between these central desert settlements.

In the opinion of one of the teachers, the education system in the desert had no appeal for the children. At every desert settlement children were not coming to school frequently enough, or staying there long enough, to achieve even a basic level of literacy and numeracy. How could they be kept at school? It was easy to theorise answers but in practice it posed insurmountable problems.

The children of Warburton and the out-stations fall into three main groups. Those who never attend school, those who remain around the settlement but only attend school several days or several weeks at a time, followed by long absences, and thirdly those who attend regularly. But even this latter group are affected by ceremonies, deaths in the camp and

Government school, Warakuna, 1978.

inter-family feuding.

Many of the teachers of recent years have been pessimistic about the future of education in the desert schools.

We are not winning! The community expresses positive attitudes towards school but only in words not by their actions. The children, not the parents, decide when and for how long they will attend school.

The school should be closed until parents agree that they not only want a school but are prepared to support it.

The parents and children see no real or lasting advantages in school. Whether or not they attend school they still have access to the same Social Welfare benefits.

I think of Warburton Ranges and the outcamps and I am appalled at the poverty of equipment at these schools. Warakuna, a school room built by the community out of bush timber sticks and grass has a box for the teacher's equipment, a blackboard and easel, a concrete floor — in an area less than three metres square. Jamieson, a low-roofed school made by a teacher and the men, has a roof constructed from pieces of remnant iron from the demolished church at Warburton Ranges.

I think back to the poverty when I was teaching at Warburton, of the text books and pencils and half used pads that I had collected from city schools in an effort to preserve the three dollars per head per child

Natives-in-law allowance, so that I could convert this saving into a duplicator and record player for the school. What had changed? The teachers then made the blackboards out of scrap masonite, the teachers today construct their own schools and write the text books for the children. Constantly the question arises in all these outback schools, the Warburtons, the Warakunas, the Jamiesons, 'How important is the school in the education process? Is the school building in fact a hindrance to education?'

Although the poverty in resources is obvious, the most serious poverty is in the poverty of the departmental attitude towards Aboriginal education, particularly in those localities where the Aboriginal population is still adhering to traditional values. These Aboriginal communities in the desert request schools for their children, but whether schools are regarded as places of education in a Western sense, or creches with the teachers providing a baby sitting service, one is not sure. Certainly, while the children are at school they are not disturbing the adults, though they are causing problems for the teachers. But while they are at school are they making any significant gains in numeracy and literacy?

In 1973 the Federal Government agreed to fund a bilingual program at Warburton Ranges, the only one in the Western Australian State School system. The State Government was required to provide the teachers to maintain the program, yet few of the teachers sent to Warburton Ranges had training in linguisitics. Most were direct from college, having done very little, if any, Aboriginal studies, and lacking in experience with Aboriginal children. These young and inexperienced teachers were flown from the city to a remote isolated school and placed in a classroom where a bi-lingual program was operating in a language the teacher had never even heard of before. The Aboriginal teaching assistant was a fluent Ngaanyatjarra speaker but nevertheless was an untrained teacher, acquiring her professional skills by observing young teachers valiantly trying to cope with cultural problems in and outside the classroom. The bilingual program received very little support from the State Education Department and its survival for seven years was a tribute to the mission linguists and the Aboriginal teacher aides. Eventually it became merely a token program neglected by the Education Department.

There is an appalling apathy for the plight of young teachers in remote areas and the physical and mental stress that such an environment imposes. The teachers at Warburton, living behind two metre high wire mesh topped with barbed wire, developed a siege mentality and were likely to regard everything outside the school and their residential compound as hostile. One young teacher awoke to find a man with a knife beside her; another made it known that he slept with a loaded rifle beside his bed.

The teachers in the outcamps fared little better. The school administrators rarely visited and when they did it was only for an hour or two. For months on end teachers lived their solitary lives in their tiny caravans, which they were required to tow back to town at vacations — six hundred kilometres over abominable roads.

It is not surprising that they make comments such as the following.

Mrs Jennings, teaching assistant with the bilingual class, Warburton, 1978.

I had no salary for four months and had to work in the store to pay for my food bill.

I was so depressed when I stepped off the plane, that I couldn't get out of bed for two days.

I get drunk every night that I can, just to forget what is outside my door.

At the end of three months I seriously thought of cutting my wrists.

Control and discipline is a hell of a problem and the trouble with Wongi kids is that they don't feel pain like whites, so you've got to hit them harder. A teacher I know uses a fan belt, another a length of garden hose because sticks break too easily.

Teachers college did not prepare me for maintaining vehicles, changing the bucket valves on water pumps, repairing a lighting generator or patching a tyre along an outback road, yet these a teacher must do to be able to survive in the outback.

I couldn't face the class any longer so I took an overdose of tablets.

The poor academic achievement of today's desert children does not fairly reflect the dedication of their teachers. There were children in these desert schools of an age when they should have completed six or seven years of schooling who were totally illiterate and had difficulty with even the most basic of maths combinations. Dedication is not succeeding and it is sad when a young teacher says despairingly, 'After two years in the school I can't see that I have achieved anything at all.'

There were times in 1966 when I felt the same self-doubt, but when I returned to the desert and saw the children I had taught filling roles as teacher aides, stores assistants, community leaders and as capable parents, I was witnessing the positive and lasting effects of education. But these adults were the product of compulsory and systematic educational programs that no longer exist in the Western Desert and several parents expressed real concern that their children would not have the skills to manage the settlements when their turn came to take over from their parents.

Absenteeism seemed to be the major barrier to education in the Western Desert and teachers wrestle with the seemingly impossible task of getting children to school and keeping them there long enough to learn. I heard teachers ask: 'Why won't they come to school?' 'Why don't the parents send them?' and I wonder if we are asking the wrong questions.

Why should these children come to school? Why should the parents make them attend? How can we involve Aborigines in the education of their children? When we can, in all honesty, answer those questions and offer a better school curriculum, a more relevant classroom program and well prepared, experienced and qualified teachers, as proof of our convictions, we will begin to succeed with Aboriginal children in the desert schools.